MODIFIED FLIGHT PLAN

LISA KOVANDA AND BRIAN THOMAS

Woodchippers and Wings
Linco... Nebra...

D1166675

This work is based on actual events, however, some of the names have been changed to protect the privacy of those involved. Many of the medical caregivers are fictitious characters based on a combination of multiple people, as space would not permit us to introduce every person who participated in Brian's care.

Book Layout ©2013 BookDesignTemplates.com

Ordering Information:
Quantity sales. Special discounts are available on quantity purchases by corporations, associations, and others. For details, contact the "Special Sales Department" at the address above.

Modified Flight Plan/ Lisa Kovanda and Brian Thomas. -- 1st ed.
ISBN 978- 1484848685

Dedicated to Brian's medical team.

If it wasn't for hundreds of doctors, nurses, and allied health care providers, he wouldn't be here to share this story.

I lived through this horror. I can take the next thing that comes along.
–Eleanor Roosevelt

ONE

....

TALK TO ME, GOOSE

Another airplane formed in the doodles along the margins of Brian Thomas's notebook. Outside the classroom window, the clear blue sky beckoned. He closed his eyes and imagined the rhythmic whir of the prop and engine as the earth passed by below him. Why wouldn't the bell ring, anyway? His gaze flicked to the clock on the wall. Last period always dragged on longer when he'd rather be flying.

He closed the notebook and shuffled his books into a tight pile. No sense wasting precious time when the bell did finally ring. His fingers lingered on the tattered cover titled, "Private Pilot Knowledge Test Questions." It crossed his mind how it was funny he hated studying for school, but could read pilot's manuals and magazines for hours.

The loud buzz of the school bell pulled him from his thoughts. *Finally!* Brian scooped his things from the desk and bolted for the door. He pushed his way through the crowded hall to his locker. As he bent to pick up his motorcycle helmet, a hand smacked his shoulder.

"Hurry up!"

Brian grinned as he turned to face his best friend, Luke. "Bet I beat you there."

They both sprinted toward the exit. Half-way to the door, Brian collided with a cheerleader toting her pom-pons. He didn't recognize the startled girl. She must be a freshman.

"Sorry." He smiled and steadied her as he maneuvered his much taller six-foot frame around her.

Luke's head disappeared into the crowd as he neared the door.

After what seemed like an eternity, he cleared the door into the crisp, sunny, South Dakota afternoon. Lucky for Brian, his bike was parked closer than Luke's Firebird. That gave him an advantage. He shoved his helmet on his head and jumped on his bike. He revved the engine of the blue Yamaha FZR 400 and sped across the dusty gravel parking lot.

He'd nearly reached the road when Luke's beat-up silver Firebird cut in front of him. The bike slid as he braked. Luke's hand extended from the open T-top and flipped him off.

Brian shook his head. *So, that's how you want to play? Hang on, Buddy, here we go.* He sped after the retreating car. Motorcycles had advantages—one he used as he weaved in and out around cars to catch up to the Firebird. They needed less room to pass.

He grinned as Luke was forced to slow down behind a slow car near a sharp curve on the two-lane highway leading from Bon Homme High. Gravel spit behind him as he steered the bike onto the shoulder and passed the cars on the right side of the road. More gravel and dirt flew behind him as he cut back onto the paved surface. He glanced over his shoulder and flipped Luke off before gunning the engine and disappearing over the ridge.

Cool wind whipped against him as he sped over the open road toward the Springfield airport. When Luke's Firebird pulled into the gravel parking area of the small airfield, Brian already had his dad's Cessna 150 airplane out of the hangar and was completing the pre-flight inspection.

"Asshole." Luke's grin belied his words. He pulled the gate open and walked up to the plane.

"What took you so long?" Brian laughed as he surveyed a fuel sample and then dumped the gas out of the inspection cup.

"Funny. Old ladies who can't drive should stay home. How long do we have, anyway?"

Brian glanced at his watch. "About an hour. Hour and a half, tops."

Luke climbed into the co-pilot seat and grabbed the head-phones that hung from the yoke. "Then hurry up with the pre-flight, Dude."

Brian shook his head. "No shortcuts in aviation. We can't just pull over if the engine quits."

When he finished checking the plane, Brian climbed into the pilot's seat. His brow furrowed as he sat down–on something lumpy. He pulled his good luck charm, a stuffed Snoopy dressed as a World War I flying ace, out from under him. Luke snickered as Brian returned the stuffed toy to its usual place in the baggage compartment behind the seats. Brian put on his headphones and adjusted the microphone. Then he leaned out the still open door and yelled, "Clear."

He pulled the starter handle. The propeller spun as the engine roared to life. Brian taxied the plane to the north end of the runway. He checked his seat belts and grinned as he looked at Luke. "Ready?"

"Always." Luke's green eyes flashed as he pointed down the runway.

Brian turned on the Walkman CD player beside him. AC/DC's "Back in Black" blared through the intercom into both of their headphones.

"We'll see about that." Brian applied full throttle and the plane hurtled down the runway. Once it lifted off, he accelerated just inches off the concrete, then pulled the yoke back hard. The plane went into a steep climb. He glanced over as Luke grabbed the dash.

"Dude, keep it up and you'll have tacos on the windshield."

Brian laughed and shook his head. "Pussy." He flew south over Springfield and the middle of the Missouri river valley as the airplane climbed, then turned north towards the school in Tyndall.

"You doing what I think you are?"

Brian grinned and turned the music up louder as he approached the field. Below them, the Bon Homme football team ran drills. Brian spotted Coach Johnson. If their school colors had been green instead of blue, he would have looked like the Incredible Hulk out there with his clipboard. He nudged Luke and pointed. "Hang on to your tacos."

The plane swooped down out of the sky. Several of the players ducked as they buzzed the field. Coach Johnson jumped and dropped the clipboard. Luke turned and craned his neck to look as they banked to the east. "Dude, I think he just flipped you off!"

Brian gave a half-evil laugh. "I'll get him to piss himself one of these days."

Luke turned back around. "Let's go see if Troy's home."

Brian grinned and raised an eyebrow. "And Sandy happens to live on the way, right?" He laughed when his friend blushed. "That's what I thought."

In a matter of minutes, the Cessna dipped to fly over Sandy's small family farm near Tabor, a town of about 400. The cows scattered as they approached. Luke leaned forward and peered out his window. "Shit, her car's not here."

Brian reached down to change the CD in the Walkman.

"Fuck, Dude, look out!"

Luke's panicked voice brought him back upright. Directly in front of them, a concrete grain silo loomed. Brian jerked the yoke to avoid it and glanced sideways at Luke. "How those tacos treating you?" From the slight green tinge to his friend's face, they weren't treating him well at all.

He leveled the plane out and flew over a farm pond full of geese. Several took flight directly in front of them. Airplanes and birds don't mix. And those geese were really big birds. His grip tightened on the yoke as he pulled the plane into a steep climb. "Hold on."

Somewhere beside him, his mind registered Luke's scream. His own heart pounded in his chest. *Dad is going to kill me if I crash—that is if we don't die first.* "Taco status? Talk to me, Goose."

By the time they flew over the short main drag of Tabor, Brian's pulse had slowed to a near normal level, although from the color of Luke's skin he might be a goner. On the edge of town, he spotted Troy's pristine white Monte Carlo parked in the driveway of a small, white, wooden house. Beside it, Troy stood, a bucket in one hand, and a sponge in the other. When he spotted the plane, he dropped the sponge into the bucket, waved, and pointed west.

Brian banked the plane in the direction of Troy's point. As they turned, Luke grabbed his arm with a look of panic on his face. "Taco emergency."

"Two minutes. Take some deep breaths and relax. Dad won't be happy if you barf in here."

Luke raised a hand to his mouth. "Make it one minute."

Brian turned the plane toward a freshly-mowed hay field. Luke clamped both hands over his mouth and swallowed as they landed. The wheels touched the ground, and the plane rolled to a stop. The scent of earth and hay, almost reminiscent of freshly cut grass, wafted through the cabin. Luke threw the door open and a stream of greenish vomit spewed from his mouth. He breathed a sigh of relief as he discovered all of it missed the interior. "Damn, that was close, Goose!"

"Birds or silo?" Luke wiped his mouth.

"Fuck that, tacos."

Luke unbuckled his seat belt and half-fell out of the plane, where he heaved again.

Troy pulled up next to the co-pilot's side of the plane in his Monte Carlo. The tall youth leaned out the driver's window and pointed. "Luke, you pussy."

Luke stood up and glared at him. "Fuck you. We had to dodge birds and silos."

Troy waved his hand in front of his face. "Damn, that stinks."

"Hey, what's this 'we' shit anyway? I was flying the plane while you were sitting there trying not to piss your pants." Brian exchanged a knowing look with Troy. A thought crossed his mind.

He glanced down at his watch. "Gotta go. If I'm late again, my flight instructor will flip a nut."

Luke put his hands on his hips. "No way am I getting back in that plane." He started toward Troy's car.

"No way. You'll barf in it." Troy raised his hands in the air as if to fend Luke off.

Brian jerked a thumb toward the Monte Carlo. "Hey, at least you can pull over. Better the side of the road than in the air."

Luke slammed the plane door shut and stalked to Troy's car.

Brian jumped back into the pilot's seat and strapped himself in. He wasn't joking about his flight instructor flipping a nut. Tate might do a lot worse. *He might call Dad.*

He taxied the plane out of the field and onto the two-lane rural highway. Brian surveyed the power lines overhead and made a mental note of street signs and mailboxes along the road. He applied the throttle and made a quick take-off. Once airborne, he glanced down. Thankfully, he hadn't clipped any mailboxes, power lines, or cars in the process, and in fact, the only car in sight was miles away.

In a matter of minutes, Brian traversed the distance between Tabor and Yankton, passing over the Missouri River where boats made an intricate design of white wakes on the rippled surface. He landed the plane at Chan Gurney Municipal Airport, a fairly large, paved airfield for a town of 14,000 people. He taxied to the fuel pumps, shut down the airplane, and hopped out to wait for his instructor.

Two men in black suits and ties stood near another plane. One of the men was tall, with a gray ponytail half-way down his back. The other seemed like a more standard issue 'man in black.'

"Shit." Brian muttered the word half-under his breath. It had to be Federal Aviation Inspectors of some sort.

And that couldn't be good.

As if to bring that point home, the man with the ponytail nudged the other suited guy and pointed in Brian's direction. The pair walked toward him. *Just play it cool.* He tried to make his face appear calm.

The guy with the ponytail, now apparent as a Native American, pulled a badge out from his breast pocket and showed it to him. "Inspector Riley Thunder Hawk, FAA. My partner, Inspector Dan Gilbert. This your plane, Son?"

"It's my dad's."

Thunder Hawk's gaze bore into him. "Got a license to fly it?"

Brian swallowed, even though his mouth was suddenly so dry he didn't know if he could answer. "Student certificate, Sir."

"Can I see it? And your log book?"

Brian's hands shook as he pulled his flight bag out of the baggage compartment, fished out the log book, and handed it to the inspector. He tried to look nonchalant as he watched the man thumb through it.

Out of the corner of his eye, he noticed the other man–Gilbert, he thought that's what Thunder Hawk called him–walk around the plane.

Gilbert crouched near the co-pilot's door. "You wouldn't be giving rides, would you, Son?"

Brian swallowed hard. "No, Sir. Students can't give rides."

Gilbert stood up from near the wheel. He pulled his sunglasses off his face and pointed at the airplane. "Looks like someone lost their lunch over here on the passenger side."

Brian tried to cover his flinch with a quick thump to his chest. "Damn school tacos. That happened while I was doing my pre-flight."

Gilbert grunted. His face remained as blank as ever. Brian wondered if they had special classes where they taught them how to make their expressions so unreadable. Maybe a bit like those guards at the Palace in London who never flinch?

Brian focused his attention on Thunder Hawk, as he jotted in a small notebook. The Native American man didn't even lift his eyes from his work as he spoke. "You wouldn't know anything about a blue and silver airplane taking off from a field near here, now would you?"

That one he could answer. "It wasn't me."

Thunder Hawk dipped his chin so his eyes looked over the top of his sunglasses. His steely stare appraised him. "Uhh huhh."

It was all Brian could do to not break under the intensity of the man's gaze. Luckily, his flight instructor, Tate Baloun, stepped out of the terminal and headed toward them. In fact, he thought the wiry man's gait quickened when he noticed the two men in black suits talking to him.

When Tate reached them, he shifted his flight bag from one shoulder to the other so he could shake hands with the two men. He gave Brian a pointed look. "How about we do some touch and go's today?"

Thunder Hawk turned his attention to Tate. "One of your students?"

Tate gave Brian a hard stare. "One of my best students."

Brian couldn't help it. He grinned. To cover, he turned his head. Tate walked near him. "Do your pre-flight."

Tate guided the two inspectors a few yards away on the taxiway. Brian couldn't hear what they were talking about, but there was no doubt in his mind it was him. Thunder Hawk's eyes met his.

They were definitely talking about him.

Once he finished the inspection, Brian climbed into the pilot's seat and strapped himself in. He debated turning on his CD player, but thought better of it. No need to piss the FAA off even more by looking disrespectful. Instead he pulled his practical flight exam book out and pretended to study the questions.

Before long, Tate climbed into the co-pilot's seat. As he did, he reached out and slapped Brian upside the head. "What are you thinking? You can't lie to the FAA!"

Brian shook his head. "I didn't lie to them. He asked if I took off from a field."

Tate snorted. "We both know that was you. You fly the only blue stripe on polished aluminum Cessna 150 in the Midwest."

Brian smiled. "Well, the blue is faded with plenty of yellow primer showing, and it has chipped white stripes." He tried to put his most innocent look on his face. "Besides, I didn't take off from a field. I took off from the highway."

Tate shook his head, and even though it was obvious he was fighting it, a smile cracked the corners of his mouth. "We need to get your training done, and soon. Before we get both of our asses kicked."

Brian grinned. He leaned out the door. "Clear." The plane roared to life.

TWO

··

A BLOODY MESS OF THINGS

As the sun faded into dusk, Brian landed the Cessna at the Springfield Airport, exhausted but happy. He taxied the plane toward the hangar near the end of the runway. A gentle breeze ruffled the straw-colored corn along the edge of the fields. It wouldn't be long and they'd be harvesting those fields, then he would have to really keep an eye out for deer. As if geese weren't enough trouble to dodge, smacking a buck on the runway would total an airplane faster than a car. He hadn't ever seen it happen, but he'd heard plenty of stories.

His thoughts were jolted back to the present when he spotted his dad, Ray, standing near the hangar with his arms crossed over his chest. *Shit.*

Brian wiggled out of the cockpit and grabbed his flight bag. Out of the corner of his eye, he noticed the flash of a blonde ponytail beside him. *Double shit.*

His mom, Trish, was with him for reinforcement. Dad stomped over, grabbed his arm and spun him until they stood face to face. The flight bag fell from Brian's shoulder and thudded as it landed in the grass beside the plane.

Anger rolled in waves from the older man. Dad jabbed his index finger into Brian's chest. "What the hell were you thinking?"

Brian pulled his arm away and resisted the urge to rub where it stung. "Huh?'

Dad stepped closer to him until the heat of his breath brushed against Brian's cheek. "The FAA? Landing in a field?"

Brian fought the urge to step away. *Play it cool.* "It's okay, they didn't ground me."

"Maybe not, but I can."

Brian turned and picked up his flight bag, but jerked backward as Dad snatched it away from him. The cool afternoon air crept up his side as his shirt rode up. Then, Mom's hands pulled at his shirt, exposing even more skin. She sucked in a deep breath as she surveyed the deep purple marks on his chest and abdomen. Brian pushed her hands away and yanked his shirt back down. "Stop. It's okay, Mom. Really. Don't worry."

He knew by the look on her face, and the glance she exchanged with Dad, neither of them believed him. But at least she didn't push the issue.

Later that night, after he'd finished his chores and homework, Brian fell asleep looking at the flight charts on the walls in his room. Dreams of flights to exotic ports filled his mind. He woke when his arm rolled into something cold and wet. Dazed and half-awake, he patted his pillow.

In the dim moonlight flooding in through his second-story window, his hand glistened black. Now wide awake, he jerked himself upright in the bed and grabbed the pillow. The thick coppery tang of blood coated his mouth. He raised a hand to his nose. Blood smeared across his face as he wiped. Then he noticed

12

the spot where his pillow had been. It was covered with blood, too. He turned the pillow in his hands. *Did I bleed all the way through to the bed?*

He tried to stand up, but the room spun and blackness ate at the periphery of his vision. "Mom, I need some help up here." Brian grabbed a towel from the perpetual pile of dirty laundry near his bed and held it to his still-bleeding nose. Dizzy and nauseated, he leaned against the bed.

Brian blew his nose. One of the largest clots he'd ever seen came out, followed by a flood of fresh bleeding. Mom opened the door and switched on the light. Her face drained of color as she surveyed him. Her mouth tightened into a firm line as she leaned back into the hall. "Oh good Lord, here we go again." Her voice pierced the silence in the house. "Ray, get the car."

Mom insisted on helping him get dressed even though he protested. It was bad enough she had to help him with his shoes and socks, but if he tried to take the towel away from his nose, blood dripped everywhere. Together they made their way down the stairs to where Dad stood with the door open. Outside, he'd pulled the car up close to the door, the harsh lights cutting white cones into the still South Dakota night.

Brian swore they must have hit every bump on the thirty-minute drive to the Yankton hospital. He tried to close his eyes as he lay in the back seat. The quiet murmur of his parents' voices filtered over the hum of the engine and heater fan. He wondered how much school he'd miss this time. How much homework would pile up, and whether he'd be better in time to make his flight lesson next week.

After what seemed like an eternity, the car pulled up to the emergency entrance. Mom opened the door and helped him to get out. Under the florescent lights, the once white towel now was a dark crimson color.

Brian shook his head as Dad motioned toward a wheelchair. Dad frowned, but instead grabbed him by the arm so he was supported on both sides, him on one side, Mom on the other.

As they approached the check-in desk, Lisa, a nurse he'd met on far too many occasions, looked up and met his eyes. She gave the trio a quick up and down glance then turned to call over her shoulder to a couple of other nurses. "The Thomas kid's crashing again. Call the lab. I'll get them into a room."

Lisa was one of those no-nonsense nurses. Brian didn't even try to argue when she pushed him into a wheelchair. Once in the exam room, she deposited him on the table and handed him a clean towel. In moments, she had a blood pressure cuff wrapped around his arm. "How long has it been going on this time?"

Brian held the towel tight against his nose. "I don't know. I was asleep. Maybe an hour or two."

She nodded as she pumped the bulb to inflate the cuff around his arm. "So, are we going to guess your platelet count? I say twelve."

Mom snorted. "You didn't see his pillow. I say seven."

Brian smiled, even though he knew it was lost behind the towel. "Might as well go for a new record low."

He glanced up as the door opened. Good. It was Dr. Kortan tonight. He liked Dr. Kortan, even if the guy still looked like he was ready to play linebacker for the Huskers. The doctor nodded in greeting as he snapped a pair of gloves over his massive hands and picked up an otoscope from the counter. He approached the table and tipped Brian's head back.

Brian tried not to wince as the hard metal of the scope entered his tender nose. Instead, he was forced to swallow the stream of blood now snaking its way down the back of this throat. Dr. Kortan made a bit of a non-committal grunt. "We need to stop meeting like this."

"No shit. It's beyond getting old."

Lisa opened a package of chemical cautery sticks and held them out for Dr. Kortan. He took a couple of them and inserted them into Brian's nose. Tears filled Brian's eyes–not from pain–but in a reflexive action he had no control over. He opened his eyes to see a face he didn't recognize. A girl.

A pretty girl.

He blinked hard to clear the tears. He absolutely did not want her to think he was crying like a little baby.

She had on a white lab jacket with a black name tag on it. He recognized those tags. A medical student. Jennifer Marsh–that's what the name tag said her name was–held a sheet of paper in her hands. Her eyes were wide, a look of shock on her face. May-be blood bothered her. But all he could think was that Jennifer Marsh had the bluest eyes he'd ever seen. She looked at the paper again. "I didn't know you could live with a platelet count of five."

Brian grinned in spite of himself. "I win. New record low!"

Dr. Kortan pulled off his gloves and dropped them into a trash can. "Idiopathic Thrombocytopenia Purpura, ITP for short. This is what happens when the body decides platelets need to be de-stroyed like foreign invaders." He slid his stool over to the counter and picked up Brian's chart. "How long have we been doing this, anyway, Brian?"

"I don't know. Thirteen, maybe fourteen years?"

Jennifer eyes widened even more, if that was possible.

Dr. Kortan jerked a thumb in his direction. "You want to know about ITP, ask Brian. He could teach the class."

Heat rushed into Brian's cheeks. He looked at her, hopeful. A little extra time with a pretty blonde medical student, with blue eyes the color of a perfect sky at three-thousand feet? *Yeah, that might make a bleeding episode worthwhile.*

But that's not how it worked out. She did hold his hand a few painful minutes while she fumbled to try to start his intravenous infusion. He'd been on the receiving end of enough of those pokes he could have probably inserted the needle for her, but she was trying so hard. The blood loss made his veins shrink, and she finally gave up and let Lisa take over. Somehow, Lisa holding his hand wasn't nearly as nice, even though it didn't hurt nearly as bad when she jabbed the needle deftly into his outstretched arm.

In the next hour, he wound up in a cold hospital bed, a plastic-covered pillow under his head, with packed red blood cells infusing through the tubing in his arm. You wouldn't think blood running through a tube would ache, but it did. Blood was cold and thick. And, it made falling asleep difficult.

Brian awoke a few hours later as Jennifer and Dr. Kortan entered the room. He managed a smile. Jennifer listened to his heart and lungs, her slender hands cold on his skin as she pressed on his stomach and checked the pulses in his feet. Brian shivered a little. Her perfume smelled like jasmine and rain. He watched her eyes until he caught the intent gaze of Dr. Kortan on him. He sighed. *Oh well.*

Dr. Kortan clicked his pen as he finished a note in Brian's chart. "We got you out of the basement, but I'm sending you to your hematologist before your luck runs out."

Brian's heart sank. "All the way to Sioux Falls? Today?"

Mom stirred in the chair beside him. "Brian Neil, don't argue with the doctor."

Brian snorted and muttered under his breath, "Who says doctors are always right?"

THREE

....

BUT I DON'T HAVE CANCER

Why was it every doctor's examination room looked the same? Did they all have the same decorator? Maybe there was some weird American Medical Association rule dictating crappy neutral colors, ugly ceiling tiles, and florescent lights. And what was the point of making an appointment if you had to sit in the waiting room and exam room for at least a half-hour each, anyway? Brian stared at the poster on the wall. A teddy bear dressed as a doctor. Mom sat in a chair near the wall, reading an outdated People magazine.

He stared at the ceiling. "You think it's always going to be like this? You know, tied to a doctor, spending most of my spare time in hospitals and exam rooms?"

Mom didn't even glance up from her magazine. "You mean you want to give up all of this 'bonding time' we spend together?"

Brian snorted as the door to the exam room opened. Dr. Hanna swept into the room, the scent of his thick Middle Eastern cologne preceding him. He slid a stool near the exam table and situated his short frame on it. He gave Brian a quick once over, skimmed the chart then ran a hand over his bald spot. "We are looking at either chemotherapy or removing the spleen, since the steroids don't seem to work anymore."

Chemotherapy? Like cancer patients? Brian's mind ran through everything he'd ever heard about it. "I can't fly and puke. How about we just yank my spleen out and be done with it?"

Mom dropped the magazine into her lap. A picture of Kirstie Alley, looking bloated in a dowdy muumuu-looking dress, smiled up at him. "No way. We've been through this before. It's too risky."

The two stared at each other a few moments. He knew by the set of her jaw she wasn't about to back down. Finally, he sighed and shook his head. His shoulders slumped. "All right, fine. I'll try the chemo. But if I can't fly, or if I get sick all the time, we're doing something else." He thought about it a moment, then added, "Or if I start going bald. I'm not wearing a damned wig."

Dr. Hanna's pen scratched as he jotted in the chart. "I will set it up. We will also need a bone marrow biopsy before we begin the treatments."

* * *

The next week, Brian found himself in another exam room—or at least he thought it was another exam room. Who could tell, they all looked the same—in another one of those horrible gowns that opened in the back. He laid on his stomach with his whole bare backside exposed as a nurse, he didn't even remember her name, scrubbed his hip with a cold, orangey- brown Betadine solution.

Another doctor, someone else whose name escaped him, came in dressed like he was on his way to perform surgery. A full mask, gown, and gloves. He stepped up to the table and prodded Brian's hip a few moments. "You'll feel a pinch, okay? Take some deep breaths and hold still."

Pinch? Brian clenched his fist as the needle bored into his hip bone. Did they make needles the size of a pencil? He bit his lip to keep from yelling as it dug deeper. There was a grinding, wiggling sensation as the doctor twisted the needle while he pushed, cutting into his hip bone. Good God, were they trying to go all the way through to the front? After what seemed like an eternity, the needle stopped.

"Okay, now this will hurt a little."

As the doctor pulled back on the plunger, a deep searing burn spread across Brian's hip and all the way down to his toes. Stars flashed through his vision as he struggled to not jerk away. He dug his fingers into the pillow and gasped.

"Almost done. Just a little more."

In spite of his best efforts, hot tears spilled over Brian's cheeks onto the pillow. The thick smell of antiseptic burned the back of his throat as he sucked in deep ragged breaths. It was over. The burn wasn't as bad, but a deep ache remained. He opened his eyes to see an alarmed look on the assisting nurse's face.

"Get some compression bandages." The doctor shoved his gloved hand into Brian's already tender hip.

A bloody hand reach up to take the bandages from her. After a few minutes of holding heavy pressure on the wound, it was finally over. Arms helped him to sit. Brian didn't know who they belonged to.

The doctor pulled his mask down and showed Brian the syringe of marrow that surely had been pulled all the way from his toes through the core of his bones. Dark, yellow, and thick. He wasn't sure what he expected bone marrow to look like, but it reminded him of uncooked chicken fat.

Brian swallowed and took a deep breath. "Don't drop it. I never want to do that again."

The doctor shook his head. "I'm doing this to a five year-old later today. She's had seven biopsies so far."

Why do doctors always think it's going to help you feel better if you know someone else has it worse than you?

All it did was piss him off.

* * *

The following week Brian found himself in a recliner with chemotherapy drugs infusing into his arm through an intravenous needle. He'd heard enough horror stories about how chemo made people sick, but so far, he'd been lucky. It didn't help the knot in his stomach go away, though. After a few hours of staring at the walls, the nurse came in to disconnect him.

"That's it? Piece of cake."

She gave him a wry smile. "I hope it stays that way, Honey."

The next morning when Brian woke up, her words echoed in his mind. He'd been sick plenty of times before, but never like this. He'd take puking through the infusion every time to the horrible achiness. It was all he could do to make it down the stairs to the couch. And that's where he stayed until a thud woke him. His older brother, Corey, a high school senior, plopped a stack of books on the coffee table near his head. "You look like ass."

Normally, Brian wouldn't let a comment like that pass without a snappy comeback, or some of the usual pushing and shoving brothers tend to do–even when they got along like he and Corey did. But today, all he could manage to do was roll over and grunt.

When he did make it back to school, stares, whispers, and pointing seemed to be the new norm. Some of his classmates even made it a point to cross to the other side of the hall when they saw him coming, like they thought they might catch ITP from him.

He shook his head thinking about it. He'd had the disease since he was two, so these were the same kids he'd played with on the playground since kindergarten. And now all of a sudden he was an outcast because he was getting chemo. Worse were the kids who didn't know him, like the silly freshman cheerleader who sent him a get well soon card and flowers, saying she hoped his cancer went away soon.

He suppressed a shudder as his doctor's warnings flooded through his mind. "Idiopathic Thrombocytopenia Purpura can cause leukemia. And chemotherapy can also cause some kinds of cancers as a side effect." What if he got the bleeding under control, just to get cancer?

* * *

By mid-week, and after listening to Corey complain every night, he managed to make it outside to help with chores. The two trudged across the feed lot, each with buckets of ground corn.

Brian tried to keep up with his taller, older brother, even though he knew he was breathing a whole lot harder with the exertion than Corey.

Brian noticed his brother's eyes on him as he dumped his bucket into the trough. He wiped his face. A smear of blood appeared on the back of his hand. Corey's brow furrowed. "You need me to get this?"

Brian brushed his hand against his nose again. A small streak of new blood tinged it. "Nah, I'm good."

Corey dumped his bucket into the trough and walked alongside him as they returned to the barn. "You going to tell Mom and Dad?"

Brian snorted. "What do you think?"

Corey jostled his shoulder. "I think you're a spoiled brat."

Brian grinned and shoved Corey, knocking him off balance. Corey responded by half-heartedly swatting him away. "Keep it up, Little Brother. Your nose is already bleeding. A little more one way or the other won't matter."

The next morning while getting ready for school, Brian spit into the sink. A streak of blood in the saliva caught his attention. He looked in the mirror expecting to see his gums bleeding, but from the front, they looked fine. He pulled the corner of his mouth open with his finger, and discovered open sores inside his cheeks. The thought of brushing his teeth made him cringe.

The bleeding from his gums and mouth sores got worse. The veins in his arms turned into dark streaks that looked like he'd written on them with a magic marker from every needle mark all the way up to his shoulders.

And the bruises.

Big, angry bruises.

Brian hated Physical Education, where shorts and t-shirts ensured every one of them were on display, too.

Life fell into a new routine. Drive to Sioux Falls, get blood drawn for lab. Stare at the walls for hours while chemotherapy drugs infused. Drive back to Springfield, by which time his body decided it hated chemotherapy drugs. Do nothing but sleep for a couple of days. Fight his way through homework that piled up while he could do little more than drag himself to the bathroom and bed. Then start the whole thing over again. And each time got a little worse. Even the hospital staff started to notice. Of course, by now he was on a first-name basis with most of them. In fact, he saw most of them more than he did his friends.

Today, Julie was the lab tech. She knew how to use a needle. How was it that some techs' needle sticks managed to turn his entire arm into an electric inferno, while others' were barely noticeable? He watched them, and it didn't look like they did anything at all different. Well, except the students. He'd figured out in a real hurry to make excuses to avoid having the ones with terrified expressions poke him. One actually dropped the tubes, her hands shook so much.

Brian threw his backpack into a chair and rolled up his sleeve as Julie pulled her gloves on. She must be close to his mom's age, and reminded him a lot of her. No-nonsense, but she always managed to make him smile. She tied the tourniquet around his arm and slapped the inside of his elbow a couple of times. He shook his head and gave a pained expression. "Beating on me again?"

Julie stuck her tongue out at him. "Someone's got to do it."

LISA KOVANDA AND BRIAN THOMAS

He grinned. "Yeah, but you enjoy it."

She deftly inserted the needle into his arm and blood gushed to fill the tube. In a matter of seconds, she had the tourniquet released, the needle in the disposal box, and her fingers applying pressure to the insertion site. While she fumbled with the Band-Aid, her grip slipped a bit. Blood seeped around her gloved fingers. "Oops." Julie reapplied pressure and bent his arm to help stop the bleeding. "Maybe you should wait until I run this."

The concern on her face didn't escape Brian. He nodded and took his backpack to the waiting area right outside the door. He pulled out his pilot's exam study guide and Walkman while he waited. In a few minutes, Julie tapped his shoulder and handed him a sheet of paper. She shook her head. "I've seen your counts a whole lot worse."

"Yeah, but this is getting old." He stared at an aerial picture of a farm on the wall for a few moments. "If it was working, that would be one thing."

Julie swooped in and gave him a quick hug, the faint scent of her floral perfume mingled with antiseptic lingered after she stood back up. "Maybe there are other options?"

Brian shrugged.

* * *

Ray took a deep breath and touched his son's shoulder. Brian lifted a bruised arm and pulled the headphones from his ears as he looked up from his cereal. "I don't want you riding that motorcycle of yours while your platelet counts are so low."

Brian shook his head. "So the ITP wins and I lose all control over my life? I don't think so."

Ray stepped back and sighed. Brian had always been so independent. Taught himself how to ride Corey's rusty red bicycle when Trish vetoed getting him a bike of his own. Same thing with riding a motorcycle. He'd come back from combining one fall day and thought it was Corey out riding up and down the gravel section of road around their farm, and had been shocked when it was Brian who pulled the helmet off his head. Now he watched as Brian grabbed the same helmet from the counter and tore out the door. The sound of the motorcycle engine and gravel spitting filled the house as he drove off.

* * *

Brian fed quarters into the pop machine outside the lunchroom and pushed the Mountain Dew button. The can dropped into the slot with a resounding thunk. He fished it out with one hand as he reached into the coin return with the fingers of the other. It came up empty. He shook his hand and tried again as Luke walked up behind him.

Nothing.

Brian's brow furrowed. He should have a dime back. "Hey, is there change in there?"

Luke's eyebrow rose, but he looked in the coin return, fished out the dime, and handed to him. "What gives?"

Brian took a gulp of the Mountain Dew then flexed his fingers a few times. "My hands are numb."

Concern flooded Luke's face. "Is that normal?"

"How the hell am I supposed to know?" Brian gave an ironic laugh.

"Dude, you look like ass." Luke nudged him and pointed to his bruised, needle-marked arms. "Or a heroin addict."

Brian took another swig of Mountain Dew and let out a huge sigh. "Heroin addict might be more fun."

FOUR

....

GROUNDED

Brian threw his book bag, keys, and motorcycle helmet on the kitchen counter as he walked past. Mom turned from the sink. Soapy water dripped from her hands as she reached for a towel. He knew the look on her face. Distant and sad. She knew something–and whatever it was, he most likely wouldn't like it. She picked up an envelope from the counter and handed it to him. Her voice caught. "I'm so sorry, Honey."

Brian's hands shook as he pulled the sheet of paper from the envelope. His ears rang, and heat flushed into his face. "We regret to inform you that due to uncontrolled platelet counts related to your Idiopathic Thrombocytopenia Purpura, your medical certificate has been revoked. Please return any certificates to Federal Aviation Administration, Aerospace Medical Certification Division, AAM-300 , CAMI Building , 6500 S. MacArthur Blvd, Oklahoma City, Oklahoma 73169 "

He threw the paper on the counter, grabbed his helmet and keys, and stormed out the door. Somewhere, his mind registered Mom's voice calling after him, but all Brian could think was he had to get out of there.

At first, he just rode, not even mindful of where he was. Nothing but the growl of the engine, the vibration of the pavement beneath him, and the rhythmic swirl of wind as it whipped past him. Eventually, Brian stopped at the marina overlooking the wide sprawl of the upper Missouri river before it reached Gavin's Point Dam. He parked the bike and wandered out to sit. The cool breeze brushed against his hair as he stared out over the water and surveyed the Nebraska bluffs on the other side.

The thought flashed across his mind that it wouldn't take much to let the rushing water pull him under and drown what remained of his soul. *They can't take flying away from me.*

It was all that kept him going through the bleeding, the chemo, with all the horrible side effects. Knowing that for those precious few hours, he'd soar with the eagles. His dad was a pilot. So was his mom. His oldest brother, Dana, had left home for the Air Force when he was in second grade. *It isn't fair.*

He absent-mindedly picked up a rock and tossed it a few times in his hands, then threw it as hard as he could into the river. His eyes stung with tears, but even alone, he refused to let them fall. Brian took in a deep breath. He knew where to go. The only place in the world he *could* go.

By the time he reached the Springfield Airport, darkness had already fallen. His headlight cut a deep cone into the moonless night. Brian slid the corrugated steel hangar door open and caressed the side of the plane as he approached the cockpit door. He reached inside, turned the master switch on and flipped a couple of switches on the dashboard. Behind him, the runway lights turned on. Two long rows of white cut the surrounding corn field in a swath. He walked out to the airstrip and sat in the center of the asphalt runway and stared into the distance. Brian had no idea how long he'd been there, nothing but the gentle breeze rustling the cornstalks when movement disturbed the air. Dad patted his shoulder as he sat down beside him. His deep voice softened. "You can't keep a good pilot down."

Brian scoffed. "Tell that to the FAA."

Dad shook his head and laughed. "Not like I've ever known you to follow the rules."

"This time, I might have to."

Dad's big palm clapped his shoulder again. "You'll beat it. If anyone can find a way, it will be you."

"I'm cursed. We hoped one day I'd outgrow it, and I'd be normal. Now I'm older, and things keep getting worse."

FIVE

....

THE GAMBLE

Another exam room. The only thing that made this time different was both of his parents occupied chairs along the wall. And both of them were staring at him. What? Was he supposed to say something profound? He jammed his headphones on and closed his eyes.

Finally, Dr. Hanna came through the door. He silently ruffled through the pages of the chart a few minutes before coming to the table. He examined Brian's hands then extended his index and middle fingers to him. "Squeeze."

Brian gripped the doctor's fingers. Dr. Hanna's brow furrowed. "How long have they been like this?"

Brian shrugged. "About a month."

Dr. Hanna shook his head and made some notes in the chart. "We are running out of options, and your ITP is out of control."

Mom spoke, exasperation tinged her voice. "What are we supposed to do? Give up?"

Dr. Hanna flipped some pages in the chart. "We haven't tried Rituxan or Win Rho yet."

"Great. More syringes full of empty promises." Brian's shoulders slumped. He'd had about enough of the drugs and all of their side effects to last him a few lifetimes.

Mom shook her head. "Either of those drugs could kill him."

"So could the ITP." Dr. Hanna nodded.

None of the adults so much as looked in Brian's direction. It was as if he'd become suddenly invisible. *This is my life you're deciding here!*

Brian raised his voice, "What about taking my spleen out?"

Dr. Hanna turned toward him. "That is another option."

Brian raised an eyebrow and looked at his parents. The two exchanged glances. It was Dad who spoke first. "My cousin Daryl died during a splenectomy. I don't like it."

Dr. Hanna nodded in agreement. "There is a risk of bleeding during the surgery. And, he'll have an increased risk of infections for the rest of his life if he decides to have his spleen removed."

If *he decides*. The words swam through Brian's thoughts. It was a subtle shift in power, but he'd take it.

Mom stood up and paced, her arms folded across her chest. Brian knew her well. She hadn't said no, and she was at least considering it. He took a deep breath. "Mom, I could get cancer or die from chemotherapy, too."

She ran a hand through her ponytail and sighed. "If the drugs don't work, you quit taking them, or change them. Taking your spleen out is forever."

"It could cure me, and if it doesn't work, I guess we go back to needles."

Dad stood and touched her shoulder. "Trish, what do you think?"

34

Mom wiped tears from her eyes. "I hate it. That's what I think. But, it's not my life, is it?"

As Dad kissed her forehead, his eyes met Brian's. He gave the slightest of nods.

Brian hadn't even realized he'd been holding his breath until he drew in a deep draught of air. Nervous anticipation washed over him, mixed with a glimmer of hope.

* * *

Brian lay on the transport gurney in Sioux Valley Hospital, in one of those thin hospital gowns, and a paper cap on his head. An IV dripped into his arm. Dad bent down and gave him a quick hug. Mom kissed his cheek. Behind them, Corey made faces at him. Brian stifled the urge to laugh.

"It's Friday the 13th, you know. Let's stay away from bad luck." Dad shook a finger at him.

Corey made stabbing motions behind Dad's back until Mom noticed and smacked him.

Brian snorted. The nurse slid his chart under the edge of his mattress and pushed the cart toward the elevator. The pre-op hypo must have been kicking in a little bit, because the whole thing seemed a bit fuzzy to him. He looked up at Dad. "I make my own luck. See you on the other side."

Brian learned something about having surgery. The first few days you spent either in pain counting down the time until you could have a pain shot, or in a doped-up daze from the pain shot. There wasn't anything much in between. Unless you counted the laps he walked around the nurses' station. Something about preventing complications is what his nurse, an old battle-ax woman who apparently got her nursing license from the Nurse Ratchett School of Nursing, told him.

* * *

Trish stretched and tried to get comfortable in the recliner at Brian's bedside. She adjusted her blankets and pillows. Gentle snores came from the hospital bed. At least one of them was sleeping. But, she was glad to see him rest. It never got easier to watch your baby in pain—even when your baby was now a six-foot tall teenager.

Light crept in from the hall as Ray opened the door and came in, a paper coffee cup in his hands. "We should head home, don't you think?"

She looked up at him, surprised. "I'm not going anywhere."

"You need some sleep, and he's doing fine. He'll be all right until we can drive back up tomorrow."

"He might wake up and need me." Trish glanced over to make sure Brian was still sleeping and lowered her voice, "And what if he starts bleeding? I'm not leaving."

Ray crossed his arms and glared at her. "I need you, too."

Was he serious? She stared at him, incredulous. "Now you're being ridiculous."

Color flooded up his neck and spread across his face. His voice rose. "He's fine. You've got another son at home, and a husband who needs you, too. Don't we count?"

She tried to shush him, but it was too late. Brian's voice, thick with sleep and pain medicine broke in, "Don't fight because of me."

Trish stroked his arm. "It's okay, nobody's fighting." She glared at Ray.

Ray's brow furrowed. He bent down and kissed Brian on the cheek. "So, are you coming?"

Trish massaged her temples and pulled her blankets closer to her chin. No, she wasn't coming. Not until she was able to take Brian home with her. Ray watched her a moment, then disappeared back into the hallway.

* * *

Then the bruising started again.

They'd drawn blood every morning since his surgery, and when they had trouble stopping the bleeding from the needle stick, Brian knew it wasn't good. Even before the Nurse Hatchett clone wheeled another IV pole with platelets hanging from it into his room.

Worse yet was seeing the expressions on his parents' faces as they worried at his bedside. Yes, it had been his choice, and instead of making him better, if anything now things were worse. It sucked. No one said, "I told you so," but the words still echoed through his mind at night as the annoying clatter of IV pumps kept him awake.

A few days later, they finally let him go home. And the following week, Brian was right back at McKennan Hospital in Sioux

Falls, hooked up to chemotherapy. At least this time his room had a window, so he had something to look at.

The heavy thump of rotors vibrated the glass as a medical helicopter landed on the helipad directly outside on top of a parking garage. His jaw tightened. *Just get this ITP under control, no matter what it takes. It will all be worth it if I can fly.*

SIX

....

HOMEWORK BLUES

Brian rolled over enough to grab the remote control from the coffee table and pointed it toward the television. This time, he not only had the horrible fatigue that accompanied chemotherapy, he also had the pain and discomfort that followed a major surgery to contend with.

His arm brushed across the row of staples that ran from directly below his sternum to his belly button. He'd thought about putting on a shirt when he got up, but decided against it. Lifting his arms up enough to get a T-shirt over his head was too painful. It wasn't worth the effort to go lie on the couch, anyway.

Brian glanced down at the wound. Dark bruises rimmed the edges. Some were turning a putrid shade of green that reminded him of a bad Frankenstein costume. He was back on steroids, and they kept him awake. The constant state of sleep-deprivation was like barely existing, not really being alive.

Behind him, a door opened, and Corey came into the living room. He carried a stack of books in his arms reaching nearly to his chin. He dumped them on the coffee table in front of Brian. "Hey, Little Brother, I brought you a present."

An overwhelming sense of defeat crept through Brian as he stared at the pile. Sarcasm dripped through his voice, "You did it all for me? What a great get-well present."

Corey snorted and grabbed a video game controller from the television stand. "Hell no. I didn't even want to carry it all home. You owe me."

Brian lifted the cover of the geometry book on the top of the pile. Inside was a list of assignments, all neat and typed out for him. He stared at it, not really registering much, then sighed and closed it.

Maybe tomorrow.

Or the next day.

* * *

Unfortunately, that's what Brian told himself every day, until he ended up back at school, with the same stack of books, and no completed homework.

His teachers were unimpressed.

He knew this because they sentenced him to detention every night until he got caught up. So, here he sat, as the clock on the study hall wall ticked over to 4:15, with a pile of books strewn across his desk. At the rate he was going on things, he might get out of detention by the time school got out for the summer.

Maybe.

Something whacked Brian in the back of the head, and a paper football fell onto the top of his books. He turned around to see Luke, who'd managed to get a detention totally unrelated to homework–no surprise there–grinning.

"Asshole!" Brian mouthed the words at him so the detention teacher, Mr. McCloud, wouldn't hear.

Luke flipped him off in return.

Both he and Luke turned their attention back to their desks as the music teacher cleared his throat. "Luke, you want to be back in detention tomorrow, too?"

"Not really."

"Then stop distracting Brian. I'm sure he doesn't want to be here any longer than necessary, either."

Brian stared at the pile of books and muttered under his breath, "No shit."

Mr. McCloud stood up from his desk and walked close to him. He leaned down and placed his hands on either side of Brian's desk. "You've been back in school two months now. You're lucky you didn't get all zeros."

Brian scowled. "Sorry I didn't think more about homework while I was having surgery and taking chemotherapy."

Mr. McCloud's deep blue eyes bore into his. "You can use that as a cop out if you want, but somehow I never took you for the type to go for the easy way out."

Brian stared at the stack of papers and books on his desk and sighed. He grabbed his pen and opened a book. He was right.

Dammit.

* * *

It wasn't just the homework that dealt him fits.

Brian slammed the kitchen door and threw his helmet and book bag on the counter. Apparently, it didn't faze Mom much.

She continued to stir the spaghetti on the stove. "Corey had to do your chores again."

"It's not my fault!" Frustration sounded in Brian's voice.

"Oh? And whose fault is it?"

He plopped down in a chair at the kitchen table and shook his head. "The office got all pissed. I didn't have a note when I needed to leave for chemo."

Mom straightened and turned toward him. Fire snapped in her eyes. "Well, that's bullshit. I'll fix it." She grabbed a piece of paper and pen from the counter. Her hand flew as she scribbled the note. "Here. 'Brian Thomas has my permission to write his own excuses from class for medical reasons. His parents work to pay for his treatment and aren't always available to do it for him.' That ought to do it." She handed him the note and grabbed the spaghetti pot, which was now boiling over onto the stove.

Brian grinned as he folded the note and placed it carefully in his book bag. Things might be looking up.

* * *

The look on the school secretary's face when he handed her the note was about priceless. He thought her eyes were going to bug right out of her head. Brian grinned as he headed to his locker. Finally, some power over his own life.

Someone tapped on his shoulder as he pulled his history textbook from his locker. He turned, expecting the principal, or another of the office staff. Instead, he found himself facing Mr. McCloud. The music teacher raised an eyebrow. "Heard you got all of your make up work done, Thomas."

Brian shook his head and chuckled under his breath. "Detention sucks. No offense or anything."

Mr. McCloud laughed. "None taken. That's the general idea, anyway. How goes the pilot's license? I kind of miss watching you flying over town."

Well huh. This guy might be a little cooler than he'd given him credit for. "Still in a holding pattern while I wait for the FAA to decide on my medical certificate. I have to file an appeal when my health turns around."

"Sounds worse than detention."

Talk about an understatement. "A lot worse."

SEVEN

....

TURBULENCE

Unlike detention, waiting for the FAA was a sentence with no parole date. After a few weeks, Brian went from rushing home to grab the mail, to not even caring enough to look through the pile on the counter every day. He had no reason to expect today to be any different. Yet, there it was. A thin letter propped up on the stove, addressed to him. It looked exactly like the one he'd received to strip him of his medical certificate. Brian gave a wry grin as the irony struck him.

His hands shook a moment as he turned the envelope over. He blew out a deep breath, then ripped it open. "Authorization for Special Issue of Medical Certification. Dear Mr. Thomas, we are pleased to inform you..." Brian's vision blurred a bit. It didn't matter, he didn't need to read any more.

His fist pumped in the air. "Oh, hell YES!"

He could fly.

Brian nearly tripped as he ran to the phone to call Tate Baloun.

If today hadn't been Friday, he would have skipped school. As it was, he only had to deal with a night of restless sleep before heading off to the airport. Tate met him next to the plane. His powerful grip clapped Brian's shoulder. "Good to have you back, Thomas."

He couldn't contain what had to be a goofy grin on his face. "Let's get it on!"

Tate even let him daredevil a little bit. The sensation of flying—freedom. God, he'd missed it.

* * *

It couldn't last—the sense of everything being right with the world he got when it was nothing but him, the drone of a plane motor, and the open sky. Come Monday morning, he sat across the desk from Brenda McCarthy, the Bon Homme guidance counselor.

She adjusted her horn-rimmed reading glasses on her nose and looked up from the file folder of papers on her desk. "We've got a problem with your classes."

Brian squirmed in his seat. "What kind of problem?" He'd done all of his homework. Got everything caught up. And he'd done it right, too. Not some half-assed attempt like he'd been tempted to do at first. Study hall was bad enough, but going back every day for detention was something he never wanted to do again.

Mrs. McCarthy slid the papers past the perpetually full candy dish on her desk toward him. From the size of her, he suspected she had to fill it several times a day. "You don't have enough credits, and you're missing a required class. You won't be able to graduate without it."

Brian's gut clenched. "So, I need to go to summer school?" The words came out dry. He was looking forward to long hours flying when he wasn't helping with chores around the farm. A last hurrah of freedom before his senior year. Soon enough, he'd need to make a decision about a job or college. But this summer was supposed to be nothing but fun.

Mrs. McCarthy gave him a sad look and shook her head. "I wish it was that easy. But you'll have to repeat your junior year."

Brian sat in stunned silence as a sense of cold numbness crept through him. Then the irony hit him and he snorted. "Well, can you at least give me back all the homework I just busted my ass finishing? I'll turn it in next year." He took a deep breath and resisted the urge to shove his chair across the room as he pushed his way into the hall.

Brian threw his things into his locker. He slumped against the wall for a moment, then slammed the door shut. "Shit." He wanted to scream, but managed to keep his voice low.

The bell rang, and students flooded the hall. Luke broke off from a group of guys and elbowed him. "You going to the pep rally?"

The laugh that came out sounded cynical. Brian knew it. And he didn't care. "Fuck, no. I get an extra whole year to cheer for Bon Homme High."

Luke eyed him. "Say what?"

"I got held back. And get this. It's for half a credit hour." The reality of the situation dawned on him. He was stuck in high school while all of his friends would be heading off to college.

"You're joking, right?"

"Do I look like I'm joking?"

Luke moved closer to him, a look of concern–almost pity–flooding his face. "What are you going to do?"

Brian shrugged. "Not stick around here, that's for sure." He yanked open his locker, tore a piece of paper from his spiral note-book and scribbled a hurried note. "I'm sick. I'm going home."

"Yeah, right. You're taking you're pilot's exam later today. It's all you've talked about this week." Luke laughed and shook his head.

"Yeah, well watch this." Brian folded the page into a paper air-plane. As he walked past the door to the office, he launched it in-to the room. A sense of satisfaction filled him as it soared overhead and landed on the desk in front of the startled secretary.

EIGHT

....

CERTIFIED

Brian walked into Tate's tiny office. An old metal desk and beat-up chairs nearly filled the space. The flight instructor sat with his legs propped up on the tattered vinyl seat of a chair, a game of solitaire open on his computer. He checked his watch as the door closed.

"Boo."

"I heard you coming from ten miles out." Tate minimized the Solitaire game on his desktop, his voice calm and quiet.

Brian pulled his logbook from his book bag. Tate reached out and took it from him. He flipped through it and made some notations, then signed it. "You nervous?"

Well, yeah. But he wasn't about to say so. Brian shrugged. "Just like a first date."

"I'm going to suggest you skip the kiss goodnight." Tate laughed. "Besides, you probably have twice as many undocumented flying hours as you do in this book." He tossed the logbook back to Brian.

He didn't have to worry very long. In a matter of minutes, he was back in the Cessna, headed from Yankton to Sioux City, Iowa to take his exam. Flying always put him in the zone, and today even more so.

The weather station at the Sioux City airport reported a 4,000 foot broken cloud ceiling, but it was closer to 1,500 feet overcast. So, instead of blue skies with scattered clouds, it was more like flying in fog. The type of conditions even experienced pilots might avoid, let alone a student pilot flying solo. As long as he stayed close to the Missouri River valley, the visibility was good enough to give him a view of winding river below. He'd never actually flown this route before, which made it even better.

Brian landed and taxied the plane near the Jetsun Aviation building in Sioux City. Inside, he found George Prescott, his white-haired flight examiner, seated behind his desk.

The contrast with Tate Baloun struck him. On one hand, his tall flight instructor was at home in a military or school cast-off office. Really, it was little more than a place to stash his stuff, like an oversized school locker with a desk and chairs. His real office was in the cockpit of a plane, and it showed.

Prescott, on the other hand, looked like his heavy-set frame belonged behind his glass-topped desk and oiled leather chair. Old black and white aviation photographs adorned his wood-grained office walls.

Brian sank into one of the more comfortable seats–even though he preferred Tate's torn vinyl chairs. The ones with the tufts of lumpy stuffing sticking out. He caught himself fidgeting as the examiner reviewed his papers and logbooks.

Prescott glanced over his glasses at him. "Thomas, huh? Any relation to Ray and Trish Thomas?"

Brian nodded. "They're my parents."

"I gave your mom her flight check ride. Would have been before you were born." Prescott grabbed the flight bag from the corner of his desk. A faint hint of a smile lifted the crinkles in the corners of his eyes. "Your mom almost threw up, she was so nervous. Hope you didn't inherit that tendency from her."

Brian glanced out the window at the gray overcast sky. "What do you think, can we still fly?"

Prescott broke the first smile Brian had seen. "I think we can work with it. You made it here, right?"

* * *

The wheels of the Cessna connected with the runway in a smooth motion. Brian glanced over at Prescott, who was wedged into the tight co-pilot's seat. His face remained unreadable, like it had for the entire flight.

As they taxied to the front of the Jetsun Aviation Building, Prescott scribbled some notes in his logbook. "Well, I don't know."

As he paused, Brian's heart thumped in his chest.

"I guess we need to see about getting you a pilot's certificate."

Relief coursed through Brian. He couldn't suppress his grin as the overweight flight examiner struggled to free himself from the tight confines of the co-pilot's seat and climb out of the plane.

After the paperwork was signed, Brian handed a camera to one of the fuel truck drivers. Prescott stood next to him in front of the plane and shook his hand. Above them, the clouds broke, bathing them in warm light.

‥‥‥‥‥‥‥‥‥‥‥‥‥‥‥‥‥‥‥‥‥‥‥‥‥‥‥‥‥‥‥‥‥‥‥

NINE

HOMECOMING

Brian forced himself to go to school the next day. Even the prospect of having to come back for a whole extra year couldn't dim the sense of freedom and joy knowing his pilot's license sat securely inside the logbook in his flight bag. He made his way through the throng of students that crowded the halls and headed toward the door leading to the Senior Lounge.

As he reached for the handle, Mr. McCloud grabbed his shoulder. "Thomas, this is the Senior Lounge. You're not a senior."

Brian grinned. "I'll be a super-senior next year. Besides, the prettiest girls are in there. Homecoming is coming up."

The music teacher laughed. "I suppose you've earned it. How would the pilots' say it? Keep it off the radar, okay?"

The lounge was little more than an old storage closet that had been emptied and converted with a few donated couches and lounge chairs. In the corner, a small television sat on a beat-up table, invariably tuned to those vapid soap operas the girls all seemed addicted to watching.

He flopped into a tattered green recliner that smelled of cats. In a few seconds, Luke took a chair near him. "Sandy said she'd go to Homecoming with me. Who are you going to ask?"

Brian glanced around the room at the clusters of girls. "I think I'm going solo."

"You want us to save you a seat at the game?"

He shook his head. "I'll catch up with you afterward."

* * *

Luke sat next to Sandy near the top of the bleachers overlooking the Bon Homme football field, his fingers laced through her smaller hand. He scanned the crowd of light blue and red clad students for Brian. Even though he'd said he would meet them later, he half-expected his friend to show up.

Below him, the cheerleaders held up a big banner proclaiming, "Go Cavaliers." The football team rushed out of the locker room and ran through it as the band played the school fight song. Over the bright white glare of the field, red lights flashed in the distance near the tree line. He watched them a moment, and sure enough, they were getting closer. He nudged Sandy. "Check it out."

Her gaze followed his finger as Luke pointed at the approaching lights.

"Is that what I think it is?"

Luke grinned. "Going solo. Nice."

The whine of the plane engine sounded over the crowd. The white landing lights ringed the field like a giant search light as the plane circled overhead. Luke laughed. "Shit. We should have asked him to save us a seat!"

* * *

Brian glanced out the side window at the football field as he circled overhead. Inside, the instrument panel of the plane glowed red from the cockpit light. He squinted and shaded his eyes as the bright white lights from the football field hit his eyes and stripped him of his night vision.

Brian fished his sunglasses from his flight bag and put them on as he hit the play button on his Walkman. The deep guitar of Metallica flooded his headset. He smiled. Well, if you were going to enjoy Homecoming, this was the way to do it.

* * *

Monday, during Physical Education, Brian ran laps around the same track he'd flown over that Friday night. Not nearly as much fun running around the field as it had been flying over it, that much was for sure. He noticed Coach Johnson watching him, his arms crossed. As he passed in front of him, the coach motioned him over.

Instead of the anger he expected, Coach Johnson clapped him on the shoulder. "Nice flying, Thomas. You even showed a little school spirit with the blue airplane." A small smile cracked his face as he pulled Brian close. "But if you think you can make me piss myself by buzzing the team during practice, you're fooling yourself."

Brian gulped. His guilt must have shown on his face as the coach raised an eyebrow. "Yeah, I've got my sources." He released Brian. "Besides, you aren't the first Thomas kid I've had in this school."

* * *

Brian tossed books into his locker. Troy and Luke noticed him and came over. Troy leaned against the wall near his locker. "Stupid assemblies. At least we might get a nap."

Brian grabbed his flight bag. "You two have fun."

Luke gave him a quizzical look. "What do you mean us two?" Brian grabbed a note out of his flight bag. "Get out of jail–I mean school–free card." He smiled and flipped them off as he headed toward the office to drop it off. Way too nice a day to waste on an assembly. Not when there was a clear windless sky out there, and gas in the tanks of the plane.

TEN

....

A PLAN?

As his senior year wound to a close, Brian sat in the living room between both of his parents. It was one of those uncomfortable situations that send kids into therapy for decades. He squirmed in the uncomfortable silence as both parents stared at him. Finally, Dad breached the void."You need a plan."

"I thought a year off would be nice. I did do an extra year in high school and all."

The color in Dad's face rose. "Not an option. If you aren't a student, we can't keep you on our health insurance. One bleeding episode would bankrupt us."

Mom chimed in, "Do you know how much IVIG costs? Over a hundred grand for one dose. You had six doses once. And that's not the platelets, or the hospital, the doctor, or the lab bills." She ticked off the items on her fingers.

He really didn't know. His parents had never told him how much all of his treatments cost, and in fact, made it a point to shut him off if he asked.

Mom broke into the conversation again. "Your grades are so good this year."

Dad snorted. "They ought to be. He only goes to school half days, if he shows up at all."

Anger flooded through Brian. He fought to control his voice to keep from yelling. "Hey, I paid my dues. I've earned some free time."

Dad glared at him. "Free, my ass. Have you seen the airport gas bill this month?"

The two stared at each other, while Mom seemed afraid to say anything. She probably didn't want to get dragged into the middle of what was rapidly becoming a huge mess.

But it wasn't like all he did was fly. He did a whole lot around the farm. Plus the plane maintenance. "Well, who changes the tires and oil for you? I saved you two months worth of gas bill over what you would have paid someone else to get it done."

Brian thought his response sounded reasonable, but Dad looked like he wanted to jump off the couch and throttle him. Might have done it if Mom hadn't touched his arm. "Ray, maybe that's the answer."

Dad turned to stare at her. "What? Fixing *my* plane that I never get to fly because *he's* too busy flying it? Still doesn't help with the insurance problem."

Mom shook her head. "No, but if he's going to trade school to learn how to fix other people's airplanes it could."

Corey wandered through the living room on his way upstairs. Fresh from work, he still had on his dirty clothes. His ripped t-shirt read, *CR Industries*. Dirty factory work, something Brian wasn't interested in doing at all. Farming, factory work, or a job at the prison. Those were about his only options if he stayed in Springfield. Maybe this school idea wasn't so bad after all.

"You should take your brother with you." Dad pointed at Corey.

Corey stopped and turned toward them. "What the hell?"

Dad glared at Corey. "You've been out of school for four years. Video games aren't going to get you out of the house, either."

Brian swallowed hard. This was starting to sound like his life was being decided for him. "I bleed. Do you think a career with tools and sharp metal is really such a great idea? I was thinking maybe nursing."

Dad snorted. "There's a world of difference between nursing planes and nursing people. Ask your mother. People shit and piss themselves all day. You'd hate it."

Corey threw his hands up. "I still don't know what any of this has to do with me."

Dad turned back to him. "Your brother bleeds. He forgets to take his meds. You can keep an eye on him."

Brian broke in, "Are you saying I need a babysitter?"

Both of his parents exchanged glances, then replied in unison. "YES!"

ELEVEN

....

GRADUATION

Trish sat next to Ray in the crowded bleachers as the graduating class marched onto the football field. She nudged her husband. "They all look the same in those robes. Can you see where he is?"

Ray craned his neck and peered as the students in their caps and gowns took seats along the fifty yard line. "How the hell are you supposed to tell from up here? We'll find him after the ceremony so you can take pictures."

Then she noticed the familiar drone of an airplane engine. Her eyes darted to the sky. Sure enough, there was the tell-tale blue of their Cessna. Next to her, Ray stiffened. Trish shook her head and laughed in spite of herself. "Well, you told him he had to make an appearance at his graduation. You didn't tell him how he had to do it."

As the plane dipped low toward the field, people in the stands around them pointed and stared. Some ducked as it buzzed overhead. A graduation cap and tassel dropped and fluttered toward the football field. Out of the corner of her eye, she noticed a grudging smile form on Ray's face.

TWELVE

....

LAKE AREA

Summer passed all too quickly. Before Brian knew it, he and Corey were off to Lake Area Technical School to study aircraft maintenance. It really wasn't such a bad idea, and once Corey signed on to go with him, he was actually looking forward to learning more about planes. Maybe even learning how to fly some of them.

There were sixteen guys in their class, including him. He and Corey had a pretty sweet set-up as far as their apartment. It was close to campus, so biking was an option. Of course, they were guys, so most of the time it was littered with empty pizza boxes and piles of dirty clothes. Dad even let them take the airplane with them, making it a quick commute back and forth on the weekends.

He liked most of the faculty, especially Greg Kline. He was an older guy, or at least he had the salt and pepper hair of an older guy, and he really knew his stuff. Highly motivated and a good teacher. Even some of the classes that put his classmates into a dazed stupor, Brian liked.

The real fun came when they got to actually work on planes. Brian was fairly good at working on his dad's Cessna 150, but here they got to tear into the bigger stuff. Complex planes, with turbo chargers, hydraulic systems, and there were even some jet-powered aircraft.

* * *

Things would have been pretty close to perfect if the stupid ITP would stay in remission. Today, Brian sat in the doctor's office as Dr. Schmidt, his new hematologist, pinched his fingers. "Vincristine, Vinblastine... what's the difference?"

The middle-aged man looked up at him. "Sometimes you'll tolerate a different drug in the same family better."

"Yeah, well try fishing a screwdriver out of a helicopter hell-hole when you drop it because you can't feel it." Brian flexed his hands a few times. The numbness was getting old.

"Hopefully you'll have fewer side effects with the Vinblastine. And we'll need to start some medicine called erythropoietin-alpha. You're anemic from the chemotherapy. This will help your body make more blood so you don't need so many transfusions."

"Great. More drugs." Brian frowned. "What kind of side effects does this one cause?"

He found out the next week. Corey came home with a pizza box in his hands to find Brian sprawled out on the floor, his legs propped up on the recliner. It was about the only position that gave him any relief from the horrible bone pain in his legs. Beside him on the floor were an empty gallon of milk, an open bottle of Tylenol with some of the pills scattered where he couldn't reach them, and an empty carton of ice cream.

Corey surveyed him. "What the fuck is this?"

Brian winced as he turned his head to look at his brother. "I think I'm dying. My legs don't work, and I can't make them stop hurting. I'm pretty sure it's the new meds I'm on."

Corey prodded the empty milk container with the his shoe. "How'd you plan on peeing?"

Truth be known, he really hadn't planned on much, but once he'd finished the milk, it had crossed his mind he could use the empty jug to pee in if he really had to. Thankfully it hadn't come to that. He groaned. "Just help me get to bed."

Corey grabbed his arm and helped pull him up from the floor. Brian gasped as white-hot pain flooded his senses. He threw his arm over his brother's shoulder to take some of the weight off his legs.

"You could try calling the doctor, you know."

Brian snorted. Why? So they could give him more drugs that would cause even worse side effects? The ones he had now were horrible enough. The last thing he wanted was more drugs.

Brian learned how to plan his life around the injections. Get the shot on Friday, spend most of the weekend fighting the bone pain, and by Monday, hopefully be able to walk enough to endure class. By the end of the week, things would get close to normal, just in time to start the whole cycle over again.

At least the field trip took place in the middle of the week. He'd heard about Duncan Aviation in Lincoln, and today, they were going to get to tour the jet repair station. Even the long drive from South Dakota to Lincoln stuffed into a Ford Excursion with a bunch of other guys didn't bother him. Sure, it would have been quicker to fly, but he wasn't in charge of the travel arrangements.

The Excursion pulled up in front of the Duncan building entrance, a curved glass structure with the company name and logo emblazoned on it. Brian took a deep breath as the group was led into the hangars. Unlike most airplane shops he'd seen, this one was immaculate. Even the floor sparkled. Not a tool seemed to be out of place, and it wasn't like these guys weren't busy. Mechanics swarmed all over the planes, ranging from huge corporate jets to smaller charter jets.

A chiseled middle-aged man in a gray polo shirt bearing the Duncan logo greeted them."I'm James Prater. I'd like to welcome you all to Duncan Aviation. We're the largest family-owned heavy corporate jet maintenance depot in the world."

Brian nudged Corey and whispered under his breath, "This place is top on my list after graduation."

Corey made a face and snorted. "You don't watch football. You think you can stand all the Husker fans in Lincoln?"

Brian grinned. "I'm more worried that it isn't far enough away from Springfield."

Everything about the place impressed him. The best way to land a job there was to make his resume look good. And that meant study. Lucky for Brian, studying airplanes came easy for him. In fact, he often found himself with more time on his hands than he knew what to do with. He wandered around the school shop and poked his head into what projects other students had going on, but the real problem was all of their assignments involved tearing down and reassembling motors and plane components. Nothing real-life or broken. Not much of a challenge, just removing and reinstalling parts.

Brian finished his assignment in no time, and as his class-mates plodded through their work, he glanced at his open tool case and had an idea. He pulled the rolling case near the hangar door and opened it. Maybe a half hour passed before Greg came to check on him. By that time, he had pulled his own plane near the hangar and had the cowl off. "What's this, Thomas?"

Brian wiped his oily arms on a shop towel. "A 1962 Cessna 150. It's in decent shape, too." He grabbed a wrench and loosened the oil filter.

Exasperation rang through his instructor's voice. "I know what it is. Why is it here?"

Brian barely glanced up. "It needs an oil change."

"You can't change your oil during class time. You have a pro-ject due."

Brian pointed inside the hangar, where his project, a Lycombing O-320 engine, sat on an engine stand. "It's been ready for you to look at it for over an hour. Figured I'd get some real-world learning in while I waited. You know, stuff with tools... planes?"

His instructor's brows furrowed as his gaze darted between the completed engine and the Cessna. He stalked over to the en-gine, examined it, and gave Brian a grudging nod. "Hope you brought your own oil."

* * *

Brian noticed Corey was studying more, too. Probably didn't want to be shown up by his little brother. He'd never really had the opportunity to be on equal footing with Corey, and to tell the truth, he was enjoying a bit of healthy competition with him.

Sports had been out of the question, with ITP and bleeding episodes, even though his folks had done a decent job of letting him be a normal kid as much as possible. But the age difference and his illness always seemed to make it so he didn't have the same kind of relationship with his brothers as what some of his classmates had with theirs. A little pressure probably did help him keep his nose in a book when he'd rather be out flying.

Brian stood by his rolling tool chest making sure he'd collected and accounted for all of his tools. He trusted his classmates, but it was too easy for things to walk off and get misplaced if you weren't careful. And he didn't want to have to dip into his bank account to replace anything. He'd rather put his money into the gas tank of the Cessna.

Corey tapped him on his shoulder. "I hear class rankings are out. Pretty sure I kicked your ass."

Brian grinned. "I doubt it."

Corey nudged him. "Whatever. I studied more than you did."

Brian lifted his chin in defiance. "Bet you dinner I beat you."

"You're on, Little Brother."

Brian closed and locked his tool box. The two brothers raced to the classroom hall where a sheet of paper hung on the wall. They both jockeyed for position to read the listing. The top two names were Thomas, Brian, and Thomas, Corey.

Brian gave Corey a chiding punch in the arm. "Apparently it doesn't matter if you don't study as much, if you're smarter and better looking." He ducked as Corey took a half-hearted swing in his direction. "I'm thinking steak for the dinner you owe me."

THIRTEEN

....

DUNCAN

In spite of his parents' reservations, Brian took a job at Duncan Aviation. It was no easy accomplishment, since nearly every newly-minted airplane mechanic vied for the same few coveted spots. Within a few months, and after two job interviews, he moved into his first real apartment. Out on his own, in the heart of Lincoln, Nebraska.

Overall, he liked it. Lots going on, so never boring. And unlike school, he got the opportunity to work on aircraft with real problems. The planes came to Duncan for routine maintenance, paint jobs or interior upgrades, or because they were broken. Intermittent electrical problems proved to be the most challenging. Brian even found himself scouring the Internet after work to learn more about what issues specific kinds of planes were prone to developing. Broken planes were like puzzles, waiting for someone to find the solution.

Today Brian was working on a Cessna 560, a smaller six passenger jet. To get to his work space, he had to climb a short ladder and crawl into the baggage compartment, which was the only way to reach the portion of the plane he needed to work on. He slid on his back into the hell-hole, an aptly named narrow coffin-like space filled with wires, hoses, and hydraulic lines. He eyed the filters directly above him, hydraulic filters filled with Skydol, a purple, flame-resistant fluid. It was known to cause eye and skin damage. Not to mention dissolve polyurethane paint.

Brian reached into the tangle of hydraulic lines directly above his head with a wrench. As he twisted his wrist to loosen a nut, he bumped into a hose and dropped the tool. There was enough time before the hard metal connected with his face to know it was coming, but not enough to do anything about it. He didn't have anywhere to move, even if there had been enough time to react. The wrench connected with the soft tissue beneath his right eye.

Great, that's going to leave a mark.

Brian debated pulling himself out of the narrow confines of the baggage compartment to find some ice, or at least go to the bathroom and check the damage, but decided against it. Too much effort to climb in and out of the stupid hell-hole. Besides, what was another bruise or two?

The next morning as he stood at the sink getting ready for work, he prodded at his swollen, discolored eye. It looked like someone had decked him and given him a huge shiner. He spit blood into the sink along with his toothpaste. Another impending bleed.

Brian grabbed his helmet and keys from the makeshift table beside the door and headed out onto the deck that ran the entire length of his second floor apartment. He locked the door and made his way down the stairs to the parking lot where his Yamaha flashed bright blue in the morning sun.

As he climbed on the bike and lifted his helmet, he noticed a girl–must be about his age, early twenties–watching him from the balcony a couple of doors down from his. She brushed her blonde-streaked brunette hair from the side of her face and blushed, like he'd caught her doing something. Brian grinned as she gave him a shy wave. He pulled the helmet over his head and gunned the bike out of the parking lot.

Once at work, he removed the final nuts and bolts from the aileron, a wedge-shaped six-foot part of the wing of the Cessna 560. Now he needed help. "I'm ready to pull this off," he called to the two men working behind him on another plane.

Kevin Binkley, a guy close to his age, clapped him on the shoulder as he walked past him to grab one side of the wing. The flame tattoos on one of his arms stood in contrast against the muscled tan skin and dark gray polo shirt. Hal Dipple, their boss, grabbed hold of one end. The imposing, weathered-looking man glanced at Brian. "Take Kevin's side. I've got this one."

Between them, the three pulled the aileron off the plane and carried it to a flight control rack, a padded table with slots designed to protect the piece from damage while off the plane. Once they had the part safely nestled in the rack, Hal nodded and headed off toward another jet on the other side of the hangar.

Kevin lingered. He eyed Brian's face and arms, also covered with bruises in various stages of healing. "What gives, Dude?"

Brian's brow furrowed. "Huh?"

Kevin gestured in the direction of his eye. "Rumor has it you've been getting into bar fights."

Brian laughed. "Last fight I was in was second grade."

Kevin leaned against Brian's tool chest. "So, what's with the bruises?"

It had to happen sooner or later. But describing a disease like idiopathic thrombocytopenia purpura without sounding like an encyclopedia wasn't easy. "I have a bleeding disorder. It's kind of like hemophilia, but not really." People usually understood hemophilia, or at least enough to get by without tons of other questions.

Kevin scuffed the toe of his boot against the floor a second. "Shit. That sucks."

Brian shook his head. "Tell me about it. I've lived with it for over twenty years now. It gets old."

"So you bleed easy and ride motorcycles?" Kevin's eyebrows raised. "Hell, I gave up riding when my daughter was born. It's not worth the risk. Riding in Lincoln is like having a giant bullseye on your back during rush hour."

Brian nodded. "I hear you. Some guy rear-ended the car right behind me over by the university the other day. I almost parked my bike and took a cab home."

Kevin clapped him on the shoulder as he headed back to his own work.

FOURTEEN

AMY

Brian accepted when Kevin asked him to stop by the bar after work. Now that he knew there was no need to worry about bar fights breaking out, Kevin thought they should hang out. Brian wondered how many of the other guys at work gave him a wide berth thinking he was a trouble-maker. It wasn't like he wanted to have to make a public an-nouncement about his ITP, or anything.

They didn't stay out late, since both of them had to work the next morning. Just a burger and a beer, but it was nice to hang out with someone. He hadn't really met people in Lincoln yet, unless you counted the hematologist and his office staff as "peo-ple."

As Brian pulled his motorcycle into the parking lot the next night, he noticed the girl from before leaning against the rail on the balcony. A couple of her friends were with her. A chubby blonde, and another girl with long, almost black hair. They each had a beer in their hands, and a large red cooler sat on the wood balcony nearby. He pulled off his helmet and climbed the steps. The three girls giggled and whispered as he approached his door, which was right next to where their cooler sat.

The blonde nudged the girl who had waved at him. She turned a fiery red, but stepped closer to him and fished a beer out of the cooler. "Want one?"

Why not? As Brian took the beer from her outstretched hands, her fingers brushed his. Her eyes fixed on his face. She reached up and gently touched the bruise under his eye. "Ouch."

"It's a long story, but let's just say it was a rough day at work."

She nodded. "I'm Amy, by the way. Amy Stevenson. And, I'm a really good listener if you ever want to talk about it."

She had pretty eyes. Green with flecks of gold. Somehow, the other two girls had disappeared. Convenient? He chuckled. "You must have pretty good vision, too, by the way you've been checking me out."

Amy laughed and blushed some more. "Well, I'm moving in a couple of months. I'm buying a house. Anyway, I figured I'd better find a way to meet you while I still could."

They sat on the balcony and talked for what seemed like hours. Brian wasn't even sure he drank his beer. It didn't really matter. He liked the sound of her voice. And her laugh. The way her eyes twinkled when she looked at him.

The next night, he invited her in to watch a movie. They sat side by side on his couch with a popcorn bowl between them. He'd let her pick the movie. Some rom-com of sorts. He didn't really pay that much attention to it. But Amy seemed to enjoy it. He'd liked the way her leg brushed against his when she reached for the bowl, and how their fingers seemed to always meet when they grabbed a handful.

But, she was a whole lot more than just a sappy romantic. Brian found this out when Amy invited him to go to the races in Eagle. He'd have never guessed her to be the stock car racing fan, but she was. Knew who all of the drivers were, had favorites she rooted for, and everything. It wasn't flying, but the thunder of motors as the cars sped around the dirt track had an exhilaration all its own. As the sun dipped below the horizon and a chill hit the air, she scooted closer to him. He wrapped his arm around her and pulled her body close to his.

The next couple weeks were a blur of work and Amy. Brian found himself thinking about her all the time. The taste of her lip gloss, the movement of her hand as she brushed her hair out of her face, the way her eyes twinkled when she smiled at him. He helped her move into her new house, carrying boxes and lugging in furniture for her. They made a trip to the Henry Doorly Zoo in Omaha, and held hands almost the entire day. He wanted more, and certainly she was giving off all the signals that she liked him as much as he liked her.

That night they sat–or rather half-laid–on the couch, wrapped up in each other's arms watching television. Neither of them had to work the next day, he'd made sure. Brian pulled her further into his embrace and kissed her. Really kissed her, his intent clear. He held his breath a moment, wondering how she'd respond. Amy's arms wrapped around his neck, and her fingers laced through his hair as she kissed him back. Really kissed him back, until his heart pounded in his chest. Without a word, he grasped her wrists, and led her toward his bedroom.

* * *

Life was about as good as it could get.

FIFTEEN

....

THE START OF SOMETHING

Brian pulled out a wrench to work on the wheel bearings of the Hawker 800XP, a mid-sized corporate jet he'd been assigned to repair. He glanced out of the open hangar at the blue and white lights illuminating the Lincoln Airport runways and taxiways. One of the things he enjoyed about working the late shift was the view of the lit runway on the nights it was warm enough to have the big hangar doors open. Tonight, a cool April breeze should be blowing in, but so far, he hadn't noticed it at all. In fact, he was hot.

Really hot.

He stood up, shaking his head as a bit of vertigo struck him. He grabbed some Tylenol from the first-aid kit by the sink, washed it down with a gulp of water from the fountain, and hoped he wasn't coming down with something.

Brian headed back to the Hawker, coughing. His head hurt. And his neck. On his break, he went to the bathroom and splashed cold water on his face, which was pale and covered with sweat. It was probably too soon, but he took some more Tylenol anyway. There was no doubt in his mind that he was most definitely coming down with something now. Finish the shift, then call the doctor in the morning if it wasn't any better. Probably just a virus, and he'd be better after a good long sleep. Maybe some cough syrup and chicken noodle soup. Like what Mom gave him when he didn't feel good.

He squatted beside the aircraft and tried to focus on the bearings over the pounding in his head and his now nearly incessant cough. Kevin kneeled beside him. "You look like hell, Buddy."

Brian covered his mouth as he coughed again. "Gee thanks. Feel like it, too."

Kevin's eyes gave him a quick sweep. "Is your ITP acting up?"

Brian tried to shake his head, but the room started to swim. "Nah, I think I have the flu or something."

Kevin took a step back. "Well, I don't want to catch it. Get out of here and go home."

Brian swayed as he stood up. Kevin caught him by the elbow and steadied him. "Shit, Dude. Maybe you should call your girlfriend to come and get you?"

"Nah, I'm good." Brian wiped sweat from his forehead. The idea of calling Amy to come get him recalled too many memories of calling his mom when he was in school with nosebleeds.

Kevin gave him a hard stare. "Fine. Be bullheaded. But at least call her, okay?"

Brian glanced up at the clock on the wall. It read 8:30 p.m. Good. She'd still be awake. Somehow, he managed to stumble to his car. He pulled his cell phone from his pocket and stared at the blurry screen a few moments.

Brian struggled to punch in Amy's number. Why hadn't he put her on speed dial, anyway? He held the phone to his ear as it rang. "Hey, I'm going home from work early. I'm sick."

Amy's voice sounded in his ear. "Why don't you come here and crash?"

"I don't want to give it to you."

Amy chuckled. "That's sweet, but tell me, do you have anything besides empty pizza boxes in your refrigerator?"

He paused a minute to think about it. Hell, he didn't know. Probably not.

"That's what I thought."

Damn it. He hated it when she was right. "Okay, you win."

Somehow, Brian managed to make it to her place without crashing into anything. Maybe calling her to come get him would have been a good idea after all. Amy met him at the door and steadied him as he stumbled inside.

She placed her hand on his forehead. "What do you need?"

"Sleep."

She gave him a sharp look. "Maybe you need to go to the Emergency Room?"

Brian laughed, in spite of the achiness that pervaded his body. There wasn't blood anywhere. Hell, who went to the hospital for the flu, anyway? "I'll be fine in the morning." All he wanted to do was lie down.

She didn't argue with him, but he caught her watching him as he pulled off his shoes and pants. His eyes were closed before they ever hit the pillow.

SIXTEEN

....

THE CRASH

Amy didn't know how long she watched him sleep before she drifted off herself. Yeah, guys were tough, and they hated doctors and hospitals. She got that. Brian had seen enough of them in his lifetime to give him an even stronger aversion to them. But his color... he was so pale, almost a translucent blue. It couldn't be normal.

His movement roused her. Amy wiped her eyes to clear the sensation of sandpaper against her eyelids. Brian sat up. She rolled toward him. "You okay?"

Brian mumbled something in response. All she made out of it was something about needing the grease.

"What?"

He mumbled again, a little louder, but still not much more than garbled words. "Wheel bearings on the Hawker."

Amy reached out for him. Her fingers touched his bare shoulder. Ice cold and clammy. Now she was awake–and frightened. She jerked herself upright and switched on the light. The clock beside her flashed 11:30. Not even midnight yet. She looked back at Brian. He was drenched in sweat, his skin a deathly dusky-blue all over. She'd learned enough in nursing school that fear gripped her. "My God, you're freezing." Her words came out reflexively as she ran her hand over his back.

Brian turned toward her. His eyes weren't right. He was looking at her, but... not. Maybe he was still asleep. He turned his head toward the bathroom. "I think I have to pee."

He tried to stand up, but fell back onto the bed. Inside Amy's mind, warning sirens blared. Tough guy or not, she wasn't going to take no for an answer. "That's it. I'm taking you to the hospital." Amy's hands shook as she pulled her clothes on, then helped Brian into his. No matter how fast she tried to move, it wasn't quick enough.

After what seemed like an eternity, Amy got him into his car, and probably broke every traffic law there was as she sped through the darkened streets toward Bryan/LGH West Hospital. She even ran a couple of red lights when there wasn't any opposing traffic.

Next to her, Brian's pale, damp head leaned against the passenger door. His eyes were closed, and if anything, his color looked worse. If any cops tried to give her a ticket, all they would need to do was take one look at him to change their minds.

The Impala screeched around the corner to the Emergency parking lot. Amy pulled into the closest stall, next to a Lincoln police cruiser. The officer stood outside the car, a fist-full of papers in one hand, and a coffee cup in the other. His gaze went to them as she helped Brian out of the passenger side of the car. "You need help?"

Amy eyed his full hands and shook her head. "I think we've got it." Good grief, by the time the guy got rid of all that stuff to help, she'd have him inside, anyway. Brian threw his arm over her shoulder, and she steadied him as they hobbled toward the brightly lit sliding door.

Once inside, Amy grabbed an empty wheelchair that stood against the wall and shoved Brian into it. He'd apparently stopped trying to argue with her, which struck cold terror into her heart. As they approached the desk, a middle aged nurse caught sight of them. The woman jumped up and met them as they rounded the corner. According to her photo ID, her name was Cathy. She gave Brian a quick up and down glance and rushed them into a curtained-off area.

Cathy's athletic arms helped lift Brian out of the wheelchair and onto the examination table. "What's your name?"

Brian tried to answer, but nothing coherent came out. He was going downhill fast. Why didn't they get the doctor in here? *Who cares what his name is, just get him some help!* Amy took a deep breath. "Brian. His name is Brian Thomas."

The nurse wrapped a blood pressure cuff around Brian's arm and turned the machine on. While it inflated, she pulled the stethoscope from around her neck and listened to his chest. The blood pressure machine alarmed, a loud blaring sound in the cold sterility of the room. The curtain brushed aside and other people in scrubs rushed in. In a matter of moments, they had Brian undressed, IV lines, oxygen, and heart monitors attached to him. A man with a long white lab coat peered over the throng of people at Brian. "What's his name?"

"Brian Thomas." Cathy glanced up from her work long enough to answer.

The man—*he must be the doctor*—shook Brian's shoulder. "Brian, can you hear me?"

Amy listened for Brian's voice, but nothing more than a moan came from the table.

The doctor turned to her. "I'm Dr. Davis. Are you his wife?"

Amy's mouth was so dry, she wasn't sure she could even make words. "No, I'm his girlfriend," she managed to whisper. "He came home sick about four hours ago. He thought he had the flu." Guilt rang through her voice. Why hadn't she pushed the issue and made him go straight to the hospital four hours ago?

Dr. Davis pointed to the thin white line on Brian's exposed stomach. "What's the scar?"

"What?" Amy had to think a minute. "They took his spleen out when he was a teenager to treat his ITP."

These words sent Dr. Davis into action. "Call the lab. Tell them to rush his work, and I want the platelet count stat."

Around them, the throng of medical personnel moved at a furious rate. Amy could barely see Brian through the mass of white and green surrounding him. She shrunk against the wall. Everything was happening so fast. "What's happening? Someone talk to me."

"I don't know," Dr. Davis looked at her quizzically, "Miss?"

Oh, her name. "Amy."

Dr. Davis nodded. "Where is his family, Amy? We need them."

Her hands shook as she fumbled for her cell phone and punched in the speed dial to call them. Why hadn't she thought of it sooner? After what seemed like an eternity, Trish's sleepy voice answered. "It's Amy. Brian's in the emergency room."

* * *

84

Dr. Davis left the task of calling Brian's parents to the girl-friend. In the meantime, he needed to focus on saving his patient's life. Young, apparently healthy guys weren't supposed to crash like this. The flu story didn't match with what he saw in front of him. This kid was going down the tubes–and fast. His color reminded him more of someone who smoked two packs of cigarettes a day for fifty years than a guy in his twenties. Now that he knew there was a history of ITP, and a splenectomy, he had something to go on. *Sepsis, maybe? Acute blood loss?*

More alarms blared from Brian's bedside. He jerked and pulled his thoughts away from pondering diagnoses. "Get me a central line setup."

Cathy pulled packages open for him as he donned a pair of sterile gloves. Dr. Davis cleaned the skin around Brian's collar bone with a Betadine swab. The dark brown liquid stood in stark contrast to the pale dusky skin around it. His gloved finger prodded the soft spot in the hollow of Brian's collar bone and first rib, then he jabbed the long needle into the space. Beneath him, Brian flinched and moaned. A good sign, at least he was still responding to pain.

Behind him, Amy's cries penetrated the cacophony of sound around him. He'd love nothing more than to be able to go tell her everything was going to be okay, but right now, he needed to get the central line in–and find out why the hell his patient was deteriorating.

He wiggled the needle, slid his gloved finger over the tissue, and stabbed it in a little deeper. Not one drop of the expected blood flashed back to let him know he'd hit the vein. No telltale pop of needle piercing the vein wall.

Nothing.

Dr. Davis withdrew the needle. A stream of blood taunted him and spurted from the insertion site. Sure enough, the area began to swell and turn a deep blue. "Get some ice and a weight."

He pulled his gloves off and turned to take the chart as soon as Cathy's hand replaced his over the needle site. "Let's get him to the ICU. Call anesthesia to start a central line once we get him moved."

Amy grabbed Brian's limp hand and cried. "You can't die on me!"

Dr. Davis touched her shoulder. "When will his folks get here?" There were going to be some decisions to make. It would be better to give bad news to them in person than on the phone, or relying on a nearly hysterical girlfriend.

Amy turned her red-rimmed eyes toward him, her voice small and quiet. "They said they'd come in a few days."

His heart sank. Either there was some bad blood between this guy and his family, or they didn't comprehend the situation. But how could they? All they had to go on was the word of a girl-friend. Who knew how long they'd even been dating? "We need to call them back."

Amy dialed the phone. He took it from her. A woman's voice answered. "Mrs. Thomas, this is Dr. Davis, the Emergency room doctor at Bryan/LGH West. I don't think you understand what's going on down here. Your son could die tonight."

"Amy said he was sick, I assumed his platelets bottomed out again. We've done it a thousand times." Even over the phone, he sensed the shock in the woman's voice.

"I don't have his lab work back yet, but this is much more serious than his platelets. He's barely conscious."

His mother drew in a long breath across the phone. "We're in Springfield South Dakota. If we drive, it will take us about three and a half, maybe four hours to get there. If we fly, closer to two hours, but we won't have a car. What do you think?"

Dr. Davis looked over at the monitors attached to her son. The numbers weren't encouraging. In fact, they were downright dismal. "Four hours to drive or two to fly? I think you'd better fly."

He handed the phone back to a stunned Amy just as the team from the ICU arrived. Dr. Davis grabbed Brian's chart and stepped into the hall to give them his report.

* * *

Amy glanced around. More people in scrubs and white jackets. Good lord, how were any other patients getting taken care of? Most of the staff had to be right here. For the moment, they all hovered outside the curtain, leaving her alone with Brian. He was barely recognizable under the harsh lights, with all of the tubes and wires attached to him.

She crept closer to the bed and gingerly took Brian's hand. His fingers were dark purple and so cold. How could this be? He'd been fine all day. Maybe this was a horrible nightmare and she'd wake up in his arms any minute. *Please, let this be a nightmare.*

"Brian, I need you. Please stay with me. Stay awake." Her voice sounded so small against the beeps of monitors and hum of IV pumps.

His eyelids fluttered. "I can't. Too tired." His hand grasped hers briefly, then went limp.

The monitors surrounding him blared. My God, he was going to die right here, holding her hand. Hot tears flooded her cheeks. She ran to the curtain and pulled it open. "Someone, help!"

* * *

The bright overhead lights burned against Brian's closed eyelids, a red glow even though they were shut. He couldn't bear the white heat when he tried to open them. Somewhere, Amy was crying. Because of him, he was pretty sure. He should go comfort her, tell her everything would be all right. But he couldn't do it. His arms and legs wouldn't work right.

Sleep.

He just needed to sleep. Everything would be all right when he woke up.

Brian's ears rang, and darkness devoured the edges of his vision until everything faded to a black blur.

* * *

Dr. Davis shoved past Amy into the room. Anticipating his needs, Cathy had the intubation tray open by the time he pulled his gloves and mask on. He grabbed the endotracheal tube and laryngoscope. He tipped Brian's head back and inserted the lit blade of the scope into his open mouth. In a swift move, he guided the tube between the two folds of tissue of Brian's voice box, and inflated the balloon to hold it in place. Cathy attached a blue ambu bag to the end of the tube and squeezed oxygen into Brian's lungs. *Shit, shit, shit.* He'd never seen a kid crash so quickly before. He looked at the clock and prayed Brian's parents would make it to Lincoln to see their son alive one more time.

SEVENTEEN

DANA

Dana Thomas stood near the observation window in the control room overlooking the Air Force Altitude Training Chamber. He had a new crop of cadets to train, and today they sat in chairs with masks on their faces. There was no real way to know until they hit the simulators how potential pilot candidates would hold up to the rigors that combat flight put on their bodies.

His goal, once upon a time, had been to be a combat pilot. But, he'd washed out in the G-force Simulation. Blacked out before the cutoff time. It didn't matter what his PhD in aerospace physiology told him about how to overcome the pressure. He couldn't force his body to adapt to the demands flight placed on a fighter pilot. It refused to cooperate. But, his training did ensure him a solid career working in aviation, without actually being strapped into the pilot's seat in a cockpit.

Dana's cell phone vibrated and rang in his pants pocket. He pulled it out and checked the caller ID as he answered it. *Mom?* She never called him at work unless it was important. A knot clutched his gut. *God, did Dad crash his plane?* He tried to keep the fear out of his voice."Hey, Mom, what's up?"

"Dana, you need to come to Lincoln. Now. Your brother's in a coma."

The tension in his mom's voice left no doubt things were bad. She never lost her cool, no matter how rough his little brother's ITP got.

Dad, now he panicked every time Brian got a bruise. Always had.

And, to top everything off, his plane was broken. "I'm waiting on a part. Fed Ex is supposed to deliver it later today. Let me make some calls." Maybe he could head the delivery off at the gate, so they didn't get stalled in the slow machinations of base package and mail delivery.

His mind turned with a thousand details–then he realized he was missing what his mom was saying. Something about Corey. Dana was stationed in Colorado Springs, and Corey lived in Denver. Plus, Corey didn't fly. Either Dana picked him up, or Corey would have to drive all the way across Nebraska.

"Okay, Mom, tell Corey to pack. I'll call him and let him know when I'll pick him up in Denver."

Dana fought to control the tears that made their way down his face. From the other side of the phone, his mom broke down into racking sobs. A sense of utter helplessness flooded through him. *I'm five hundred miles away, and I can't do a goddamned thing.*

"He's going to die, Dana. They have him on life support. What am I going to do?"

Dana swallowed the lump in his own throat. One so large it threatened to choke off his airway. "Don't think that way. He's the toughest guy I know."

He pushed the button to end the call, then hit the speed dial. Edith would have to maintain things here with the kids. "Honey, Brian's in intensive care. They think he's dying."

Luckily, Dana usually had a bag packed and stored in his office. His duties included responding to military aircraft accidents. Since you never knew when those calls would come, he had to be ready to go at a moment's notice. Today, it came in handy.

After another phone call to the Base Commander, he collected his gear along with the package. Once in the hangar, Dana threw on jeans and a T-shirt and ripped open the box containing the part for his Cessna 172. The cowl was already off and the engine exposed, which would shave a lot of time off the repair. He grabbed his tools and went to work.

EIGHTEEN

······································

A LURKING TERROR

Brian opened his eyes. Where was he? Something had happened, but for the life of him, he couldn't remember what it was. He peered through the darkness for a clue. His fingers rested on something soft. A sheet, perhaps? Yes, that had to be it. He was in a bed. But what bed? He tried to sit up, but discovered he couldn't move. Brian struggled against whatever unseen force held him pinned to the bed to no avail. He tried to yell, but no words came out, either.

Maybe he was dreaming? But it didn't seem like any dream he'd ever had before, and he was awake. He knew it. His pulse quickened in his chest. No, something was definitely not right.

His eyes darted around the dark space, seeking something–anything to explain what was happening. Movement directly above him caught his attention. He strained to make his eyes focus on whatever it was.

From the shadows, a dark creature emerged. Brian's breath caught in his chest. Some type of horrible monster hovered near the ceiling. Skeletal and hungry, it's sunken black eyes trained on him like it was waiting for something. A scream formed deep inside of him, but no matter how hard he tried, no sound came out.

Unable to tear his eyes away from the hideous creature, Brian searched his mind for some explanation of how he had come to be in this place. He remembered bright lights and a hard table. An emergency room? How had he gotten from the hospital to this place? He tried to turn his head, but again, nothing happened.

A sickening thought occurred to him. Maybe they thought he was dead, and he was wrapped in a shroud, so he couldn't move. *Help, I'm not dead!* Brian's mind cried out the words he couldn't form.

What if he really was dead? What if the–thing–above him was a demon sent to drag him to Hell? If it was, why was it waiting? He'd been to church, even been confirmed. Wasn't there supposed to be a bright light? A tunnel of some sort? Weren't his loved ones supposed to meet him and take him to see Jesus? He hadn't been any more wicked than any other people he knew.

Maybe they were all wrong, and this was what death really was. An eternity unable to move while black eyes bored into your soul. *Stop looking at me!* Brian's mind screamed at the monstrosity hovering above him.

Watching.

Waiting.

NINETEEN

··

CONVERGING ON LINCOLN

Trish pulled off her headset and hung it on the yoke of the co-pilot's seat of the 1968 Cardinal. She rushed to climb out of the four-seat high-wing plane parked in front of Duncan Aviation in Lincoln. The only thing on her mind was her dying son–and the quickest way to the hospital. She'd never been to Lincoln before, not once in the two years Brian lived here. The irony dawned on her. She'd always told herself there was going to be plenty of time.

As Trish rounded the tail of the plane, she spotted Dana, Corey, and Amy, standing by the entrance to Duncan. *Thank God Dana's here.* Even though she'd been a nurse for fourteen years, today she needed to be Mom. And let someone else make sense of the medical details. Lord knew, Ray would be too emotional to be much help with the decisions they might face. She'd always been the rock, not him.

Trish rushed over to the three. Before she had time to think, she flung her arms around her oldest son. Dana flinched and paused a moment before wrapping his sturdy arms around her.

Even he was used to her being the strong one, and no military training could erase it. Trish motioned for Corey, and pulled him into a tight embrace as well. Her breath caught in her throat. Was this going to be how it was from now on? Would she ever get to hug all three of her boys at once again? Tears overtook her.

Corey patted her shoulder. He kept repeating the words, "It'll be okay, Mom. It'll be okay," but she didn't know who he was trying to convince, her or himself.

Trish caught sight of Amy, standing off to the side. Brian's girlfriend's nervous glance darted between the three of them and the plane, where Ray pulled hastily packed suitcases out of the baggage compartment. The poor thing, she'd been here all by herself for hours now, waiting for them to get here. Trish broke herself away from her sons and hugged the stiff girl. She ran a hand over Amy's hair and whispered in her ear, "Thank you." Tears welled up again. "For everything."

Amy sagged against Trish's shoulder and wept. How long had Amy been awake by now? What time was it? It was dark when they'd gotten the first call from the emergency room. Now the sun stood nearly overhead.

Trish released Amy and squared her shoulders. They could talk about everything once they got to the hospital.

Where was Ray, anyway? She turned to look for him as a man stepped out of the Duncan Aviation building. He cleared his throat as he approached. "I'm James Prater, one of Brian's bosses. Don't worry about your planes, we'll take care of them." The man reached out and shook Dana and Corey's hands. He gave Trish and Amy solemn nods. "Let me know if there's anything you need."

Dana nodded. "You don't know how much we appreciate this."

Brian's boss glanced at the ground. "You just tell him to get better quick." His voice caught and he looked away. "He's a good guy."

TWENTY

....

SHOCK

As they stood in the crowded elevator leading to the intensive care unit, Trish's heart pounded as if it might explode right out of her chest. Amy warned her it was bad, but she needed to see for herself. *Why does this damned elevator have to stop on every single floor?*

Trish had to keep herself from jumping out and running up the steps. Hours had passed since Amy's first phone call. There was the blur of packing–if you could count throwing a few things into a bag and running for the airport as packing–and the absolutely painful flight where all she could do was sit and will the plane to go faster. Now they were so close, but stuck in a God-forsaken elevator.

The minute the door opened on Brian's floor, Trish darted through it and sprinted toward the ICU at a dead run. When she hit her son's room, she gasped. Nothing in all her years of nursing experience could have possibly prepared her for this. A half-dozen or more pumps stacked on top of each other on IV poles. Countless tubes, monitor wires, ventilator, oxygen... Her breath caught in her throat.

Maybe she had the wrong room. This couldn't be her son. The man in the bed had the same color hair, but nothing else even resembled her Brian. His swollen face and exposed hands were so darkly mottled they were a bluish-purple, almost black.

Trish inched her way closer to the bed. The hiss of the ventilator and clatter of the pumps attached to the unmoving figure in the bed muffled her footsteps. Her hand shook as she reached out to touch him. *Please, let this be a mistake.* She flinched as her fingers grazed the ice cold skin. Her eyes caught the plastic name band attached to his wrist. It refused to lie to her. *Thomas, Brian N, age 25.*

Hands caught her as her knees buckled. Trish turned and clung to Dana. Behind her, Ray, Corey, and Amy stood in shocked silence. Together they took in Brian's appearance.

An image of Brian as he climbed out of the pilot's seat in their plane flashed through Trish's mind. His quick smile, a flash of devilishness in his eyes. Those same lips were now blue and cracked. His features distorted by tape and ventilator hoses.

Every fiber of Trish's being wanted to pull Brian into her arms and cradle him against herself. Find some way to wrap him in a cocoon and shield him from all of this. She hadn't been able to protect him for a long time. Maybe never. Not like with Dana and Corey, where a kiss could fix nearly every scrape, and a rocking chair and some hot soup remedied every illness.

She'd sacrificed her innocence when Brian was diagnosed with ITP. The day she was forced to surrender him to an anonymous multitude of people in white coats. Entrusting someone else with the well-being of her child.

Hot tears burned Trish's eyes as they forced their way down her cheeks. Someone brought her a chair. One of those hard, straight-back things hospitals were notorious for having. She sat, vaguely aware of Ray on Brian's other side. Corey paced behind her. She had no idea where Dana and Amy were. Well, if she knew her oldest son, he'd likely gone off to find the doctor and interrogate him.

Trish took a deep breath. She surveyed her son again, this time with a nurse's eye. He was unconscious. On life support. The names of the drugs on the IV poles made her shudder, especially Levophed. What was the saying in Nursing School? *Levophed or leave them dead.* In fact, she'd never seen a patient survive who'd been on the potent vasoconstrictor. How long did they have? Would Brian wake up enough to say goodbye?

What was the last thing she'd said to him? She couldn't remember. Maybe she would spend the rest of her life trying to recall.

Some time passed, she really didn't know how long, before Dana and Amy returned with a doctor in tow. They were ushered into a waiting room, even though Trish didn't want to leave Brian's bedside.

The doctor got right to the point. "It doesn't look good."

Ray leaned forward, a look of optimism in his eyes. "His fever's gone down. That's a good sign for an infection."

Dr. Davis shook his head. "In this case, no. Because of the septic shock, he's not regulating his own body temperature."

Warning alarms went off in Trish's mind. "How low?"

Dr. Davis turned his attention to her. "We put him on warming air-flow blankets when he dropped to 92 degrees core."

Trish flinched. Septic shock. Another strike against Brian's survival prospects. Across the table, she noticed Dana's similar reaction.

Dr. Davis continued, "We need to talk about options. The odds aren't in his favor."

Trish threw her hand up as if to fend his words off. "No odds. We've been fighting *odds* since Brian was two years old. He's never played by the numbers, and we aren't starting now."

The doctor massaged his temples a moment. It didn't look like he'd slept in days. Trish knew the look. A patient who wasn't doing well could age you a decade in a matter of hours.

Sometimes less.

Brian wasn't just any patient, though. He was her son.

The doctor's gaze met hers. "I understand, but you're a nurse. We need to face the possibility your son won't survive."

* * *

Corey couldn't stand being in that waiting room another second. His breath stuck in his chest, like a thousand hands squeezed him until the air wouldn't move. Face the possibility that Brian wouldn't survive? This was his brother they were talking about. His brother who was tied to a bed all alone while everyone else was talking about odds. It wasn't some boxing match or horse race you laid bets on.

This was Brian.

He shoved his chair away from the table and stormed down the hall to his brother's room. Corey pulled a stool close to the bed and took hold of his brother's swollen, discolored hand. A soft canvas strap held it tied to the bed. Even in a coma, Brian was trying to pull the tubes out. Who could blame him, anyway?

The soft hiss of the ventilator in the background sounded a counterpoint to the beep corresponding to Brian's heart monitor. His face seemed puffier and more discolored than even a few minutes ago. Like something was rotting him from the inside out.

A few tears forced their way onto Corey's cheek. He swatted them away. "You are not going to die in here. Do you hear me? Don't you fucking die."

TWENTY-ONE

....

LIMBO

Brian's eyes struggled to focus through the bright light flooding directly above him. It was as if he was suspended above a stage with thousands of eyes upon him. Blinded by the searing heat of stage lights. *They* were out there... unseen, but waiting and watching. Waiting for something, but for what? He tried to peer beyond the light into the surrounding darkness. *It* was out there, he knew it was. Movement high in the darkness caught his attention. A flash of red eyes and a skeletal roll of extremities flexing and uncurling toward him.

I knew you were still here.

Corey's blurred face appeared above him in the cone of light. How had he gotten here? Brian's eyes darted from his brother's face to the beast above him. He tried to call out to Corey. Whether to warn him or shout for help, Brian wasn't sure, but anything to try to let him know he was here. No sound came from his throat, only a bit of a wheeze. It was quickly swallowed by a massive surge of air forced into his lungs. Above him, the monster glared at him. Anger rolled from its body in massive waves. No sound came from it, but still Brian sensed its fury. It moved from the place where it hovered in the dark and approached.

Corey's face dimmed and disappeared as the beast seemed to suck the surrounding light into itself. In moments, nothing remained but Brian and those red eyes, surrounded by the beast's hovering silhouette.

TWENTY-TWO

DON'T DIE

While Corey was at Brian's bedside, the staff made arrangements for the family to use a respite room. It was basically a cross between a hospital and motel room. Dana went with his parents to help get their things situated. That was fine, but Corey planned on staying as close to Brian's room as possible.

When the nurse shooed him out of the room to change Brian's bed, Corey took the opportunity to call home. From the waiting room around the corner, he dialed his cell phone. Hahn, or Hannah, as her American friends called her, had to be worried. "It's bad."Only a few years ago, she still lived in Vietnam, so she didn't always follow conversation in English. Even though her mastery of the language had improved remarkably since their marriage, he had trouble enough understanding Brian's illness, let alone knowing how to explain it to her. Corey paused and listened to Hahn ask again what was happening. He rubbed his brow. "I don't know how to get things to make sense."

"I come to see him. Drive?" The edge in Hahn's voice let him know she wasn't asking. It was more her telling him she was coming. One way or another.

It worried Corey enough that Hahn was alone in Denver. She was so small and fragile, as yes, many Asian women are. But this was his wife. The thought of her driving all the way from Colorado to Lincoln alone made him shudder. "No, I'll come get you. I'll find out when the next Amtrak leaves."

"Okay, you come soon. I love you." Relief sounded in her voice.

He said a quick goodbye as Dad and Dana joined him in the waiting room. Corey raised his head and placed the cell phone back into his pocket. "I'm going to get Hahn."

Dana gave him a sharp look. "You sure that's a good idea? Brian might not make it until you get back."

A momentary jolt of anger flashed through Corey. Hahn and Dana's wife, Edith, were cousins, yet the two couldn't stand each other. It was to the point where they refused to be in the same room. Was Dana poking at him because Hahn would be here and Edith wouldn't? *For the love of God, this isn't the time to get into their squabbles.*

Dad's words broke into the tension between the two. "Go get your wife. Your brother will be here when you get back."

* * *

The train car rocked with a rhythmic clack as it sped through the flat ranch lands of the western half of Nebraska toward Denver. Corey sat alone in the darkness at a window seat, his gaze fixed on the horizon, but his mind back in the Lincoln intensive care unit with his brother.

This wasn't the first crisis Brian had faced, by a long shot. Corey's mind went back to all the highs and lows of his brother's illness. Through it all, Brian had always simply been his brother. Sometimes a pest, but always his friend.

They'd managed to get into plenty of trouble, like the time they decided it would be fun to see how high they could climb in the tree outside their grandma's house. She'd about had a heart attack when she came out and saw Brian hanging off a branch. To make it worse, he'd nearly slipped and fallen.

How were they supposed to know Brian was sitting on a low platelet count? They must have been about six and eight at the time. Grandma had been a good sport about it and even kept their secret once they made it safely to the ground and swore never to do anything like that again.

They hadn't been quite so lucky with the pitchfork incident. He didn't even remember where their parents had been, but they'd left Dana in charge while they were gone. Corey and Brian had been out messing around in the barn. Brian threw a pitchfork into the air, and it came down directly on his foot.

As in through his shoe and into his foot.

Corey had to hand it to his kid brother. He'd been tough as hell when they'd pulled the damned thing out. Bled like a bitch, all over the hay, all the way through the yard and into the house.

Corey had done his best to help Brian staunch the blood flow and stash his shoes and socks in the trash. Unfortunately, neither of them were very good at cleaning up the red tracks through the house, and they'd been busted. Mom's face was about the same color as the blood that covered the floors when she burst into their room toting the soaked sock and shoe she'd pulled out of the trash.

They couldn't have been very old. Dana had left for the Air Force when they were pretty young. Even though Dana hadn't been anywhere around when it happened, their older brother took most of the fall for it. After all the carrying on about infection and bleeding, Brian had come out of it no worse for the wear. Nothing more than a silvery scar on the top of his foot. "Chicks dig scars." That's what he'd told Brian.

Brian had squinted up his face and said, "Girls? Ewww."

Ha. The joys of the days when girls had germs and the worst thing in their lives was not getting caught at whatever mischief they'd thought up. Corey smiled and shook his head. His thoughts went back to the memory of Brian in the bed at the hospital. *Hang on, Little Brother.*

TWENTY-THREE

....

I NEED A PLAN

Trish woke up in the darkened respite room. It took a few moments for the realization of where she was to hit her. The clock read 2:35 a.m. *How long have I been asleep?* Careful not to waken Dana, whose soft snores came from the foldout couch, she padded into the intensive care unit in her stocking feet and sweats.

Ray sat beside Brian's bed in the dimly lit room. Most of the light came from the mass of monitors and IV pumps attached to her son. Unaware of her presence, he stroked Brian's exposed right hand. Ray's lips moved, and the slight murmur of his soft voice reached her ears, but she couldn't make out what he was saying to their unresponsive son.

Trish laid her hand on her husband's shoulder and kissed his forehead. "Go get some sleep. I'll stay with him."

Ray's wan face looked up at her, a glimmer of hope in his eyes. "He looks a little better. His eyes are moving more often. I've been talking to him. I think he hears me."

Trish took in a deep breath and looked down at Brian. His face was a deeper purple, his nose was almost coal black. His hands were also the same dark blue, and his nail beds reminded her of a corpse. Huge reddish bruises covered his arms. He was so swollen from the IV fluids his skin looked as though it might split open. The catheter bag contained only a scant amount of dark urine. *How is this better?*

At this moment, she hated the fact that her nursing mind fought everything her mother instinct wanted to believe. She wanted to share Ray's faith. Trish searched for something to latch on to. Something to give her hope. A deep sigh was all she managed. "His hands look worse than they did when I went to bed."

Undaunted, Ray's eyes never wavered. "It always looks horrible when he bruises. Remember before he was diagnosed? When the day care turned us in to Child Protective Service s because they thought someone was beating him at home?"

Trish's brow furrowed. Did she remember? How could she ever forget? She'd been working as a prison guard at the time, and because of that, she'd been the one accused of beating their son. Why? Because she worked around hardened criminals and carried a weapon? The prosecutor had been so intent on proving his case, he'd almost managed to convince Ray it was true. It was one of many times Brian's illness nearly tore their marriage apart.

Yes, she'd always been the one who handled most of the discipline. Ray had a huge soft spot when it came to the boys. That was fine, but Trish wanted to make sure that the boys never ended up like the guys she saw every day at work. But beat her son? Never. She'd been frantic trying to convince someone–anyone–to listen to her. To convince them something was horribly wrong with Brian.

The diagnosis came as a small vindication to the accusations. All of their lives changed that day, replaced by a lifetime of uncertainty. Part of Trish's mind blamed herself. She'd spent tearful hours praying they'd find something wrong with Brian to vindicate her from the abuse charges waged against her. Fate got the last laugh on that one. She'd prayed every day since for a way to take the diagnosis away. She'd gladly go back in time and take the blame for everything, if only it would mean that Brian would never have to go through any of this.

A few hours later, she and Amy bathed Brian. It had taken a bit of convincing for the staff to let them, which seemed odd. She was a nurse, herself. *Why on earth wouldn't an RN and a nursing student be able to handle a bath on their own?* Once they had Brian undressed and the covers slid back, she noticed the increase in the amount of tissue on his fingers and toes that were black, along with his nose.

Dana paced by the door. Fortunately, Ray was still asleep upstairs in the respite room. Heated voices filtered in from the hall. Trish recognized the sound of Dr. Davis's deep tenor. "I'm telling you, we need to stay the course."

Another voice Trish didn't recognize responded. "His kidneys are failing. We stay the course, he'll die."

Dr. Davis gave an exasperated sounding sigh. "We'll put him on the mini-kidney. Give his body a chance to recuperate."

"We've got other options." Intensity filled the words of the unknown man.

Brian's doctor cut him off. "Not good ones."

Oblivious to the fact that the whole exchange had been overheard, the two men entered the room. The voice belonged to another doctor. His lab coat read Dr. Darren Michaelson. He appeared to be in his late twenties or early thirties. Apparently old enough to be out of medical school and residency, and in a private practice, at least. Trish noticed the younger doctor averted his eyes when he realized Dana was staring at him.

Dr. Davis gestured toward the new doctor. "This is my partner, Dr. Michaelson. I'll be out of town this weekend, so he'll be checking in on Brian."

Trish finished pulling the sheets up to cover her freshly-bathed son. "We need a plastic surgeon to look at him."

Dr. Davis gave her an incredulous look. "Plastic surgery? Why? He isn't even stable."

She held up Brian's black hand. "I know that."

Dr. Michaelson nodded. "I'll set it up for you." He grabbed Brian's chart and swept out of the room. Dana only gave her the briefest of glances before he headed after the young doctor.

* * *

Dana caught up with Dr. Michaelson. He grabbed the doctor's arm as he approached the nurses' station. "What are those other options you were talking about outside my brother's room?"

Dr. Michaelson sighed and put down the chart. He suddenly looked a lot older to Dana. Tired. "You've got one of the best critical care docs around. I don't know that anyone can really offer Brian more."

He wasn't going to get off that easy. Dana had been on the other end plenty of times, having ideas that older, more experienced doctors didn't want to hear. Especially since he had a PhD, not an MD. Never mind that at the end of the day, he'd been right more times than not. Besides, this wasn't some anonymous face, it was his family. Dana fought to control his emotions as he spoke. "I'm watching my brother die an inch at a time. If you have anything at all to add, I want to hear it."

Dr. Michaelson took him in a moment. Weighing him. Then he spoke. "You're the brother who's in the Air Force, aren't you? The flight physiologist, right? The nurses told me about you."

"Yes, but what does that have to do with my brother's care?"

"Some of the cutting edge sepsis treatments have a lot in common with microenvironment medicine. Have you heard about Xigris? Drotrecogin alfa?"

"Yeah. Activated protein C. But Brian has ITP." Dana's brow furrowed. The two didn't mix.

Dr. Michaelson stepped closer to him. "Yes, he does. I know it's risky. Really risky. But if we don't do anything, what do you think the outcome is going to be here? He's in full-fledged disseminated intravascular coagulation. Brian's odds of surviving the weekend are less than five percent. That's if we try this. Without it, I give him less than a one percent chance. And that's being generous."

Dana's gut clenched like he'd been punched. Deep inside, he knew the truth. He'd seen similar problems from severe frostbite in crash survivors, but his mind still didn't want to accept it. "I'll talk to the rest of the family."

Dr. Michaelson nodded and shook Dana's hand.

A couple hours later, Dana sat at the table in a crowded Village Inn facing his father, with his mother and Amy on either side of him. Their food sat mostly untouched in front of them. Dad's hand slammed down on the table, hard enough to nearly upset Amy's water glass. "You're trying to kill him."

Mom reached out and steadied it. "I need a backup plan. What we're doing isn't working."

Dana cleared his throat. "He's already on feeding tubes, dialysis and a ventilator. We've got to do something."

His father's voice raised, "I tell you, he's getting stronger. I can see it."

Mom snorted and shook her head. The four exchanged uncomfortable glances. Finally, Dad turned to Amy, who up to this point had been nearly mute in the discussions. "Amy, you haven't said anything yet. What do you think? You have a say in this, too."

Amy pushed the food around with her fork, her eyes puffy and red. "What if the treatment kills him?"

Dana nodded in agreement. "It might. We know that. But, as I see it, we don't have anything to lose by trying."

Dad scrubbed his hands through his hair. "Corey's not due back until Sunday. We can't do this without him."

Mom's ponytail whipped from side to side as she shook her head. "We've been through this. We don't have until Sunday, and I don't want to call Corey while he's driving to get back here."

Amy's small voice cracked as she broke in, "He could be gone anyway. Even if his body survives."

Her words plunged the group into silence. She'd voiced the unspoken thing none of them wanted to acknowledge. Dana had pushed the thoughts of what was happening inside his brother's body to the back of his mind. He knew the gangrene creeping up Brian's extremities had to mirror a similar process with his internal organs, including his brain. What if he did survive? Would it be worse than death? Dana didn't want to think about it.

Mom broke the pensive void. "If he dies, are we burying him in Lincoln?"

Dad scowled at her, as a broken expression clouded his face."Stop! I won't listen to you planning our son's funeral like he's already dead."

A sudden flood of exasperation overtook Dana. He slammed his hand on the table. "We *do* need to talk about it, and Springfield Cemetery overlooking the airport. How could you even consider burying him any place else? I've had that written into my burial instructions for the military ever since I joined up."

He might not have been flying combat missions, or traipsing into Afghanistan and Iraq with assault rifles, but Dana was a military man, nonetheless. The possibility of his own mortality was something he'd been trained to face since he was a recruit right out of high school. Funny, how he could face the possibility of his own death with little more than a second thought, but thinking about his brother's took so much effort.

Only a few hours later, the family gathered at Brian's bedside. Dana and Trish listened to Dr. Michaelson explain risks and benefits of the treatments. Together, they signed consent forms.

Amy and Ray suspended foam airplanes from the ceiling above Brian's bed. Amy brought Brian's Aviator Snoopy from his apartment, and she placed it near his blackened hand. Dana shook his head. It wasn't likely Brian had any awareness of what they were doing, but it gave them all something to do–and that beat sitting there helpless.

Dr. Michaelson pushed another IV pole with bags dangling from it into the room. He exchanged glances with everyone. "This is the moment of truth. Are we ready?"

It was Dad who answered, his voice gruff and choked with emotion. "Let's do it."

Dr. Michaelson inserted a needle into the tangle of tubes that already fed into the central line near Brian's collar bone. He switched on the pump and adjusted the clamps. "I'll stay close." The doctor nodded again and left them alone to wait and watch.

* * *

In the hours that followed, they all took turns sitting at Brian's bedside. Even though no one said it out loud, Dana was fairly certain they were all thinking the same thing. *I don't want him to die all alone.* He'd come in to let Dad stretch his legs. He was pretty sure unless one of them forced him to get up, Dad would do nothing but sit there and rub Brian's hand. Most likely without stopping to eat or go to the bathroom.

Later that night, Dana paced the darkened ICU and watched the monitors attached to his brother. So far, things didn't look any worse. No better, but no worse. From the corner of the room, Dad let out a loud snore and turned in the recliner he'd fallen asleep in a few hours before.

In the early morning, Amy and Mom came in to change the sheets on Brian's bed and bathe him. Now his legs were mottled purple and red. Large blisters oozed on his arms and legs. If–*if* he survived this–the road to recovery was going to be hell.

TWENTY-FOUR

BLACK AND BLEEDING

The dark monster hovered over Brian's face. From the recesses of skeletal sockets, red eyes flashed with anger. Paralyzed and helpless below it, Brian could do nothing but stare in terrified silence as it oozed blood from its body. Heavy red-black splats that dripped onto his bed.

TWENTY-FIVE

··

AT WHAT COST?

The drive back to Nebraska from Colorado was worse than the Amtrak trip. Corey called every few hours and talked to Mom, but he knew from the tone of her voice there was more going on than she was telling him. He drove as fast as he could, and wished he'd remembered his radar detector. They ate in the car while the miles of road disappeared behind them. It was hard enough to stop when forced to get gas and use the restroom. Hahn was nearly as anxious to get to Lincoln as him, which made it easier to keep pushing on.

When they reached the hospital, Corey had to practically run to keep up with Hahn, even though he was a good foot taller than his wife. When she saw Brian, Hahn gasped and threw herself into his arms, her head buried against his chest. Corey's jaw clenched as he stared at his brother. *Why didn't anyone tell me?* His voice came out much louder than he'd anticipated. "What the fuck?"

Corey stormed into the waiting room where his parents, Dana and Amy sat. Hahn trailed behind him, sobbing quietly. He stared at Dana. "What the hell are you doing?"

Dad looked up at him. "We told you he looked worse, but his vitals are a little better than they were last night."

Corey shook his head gave a hysterical laugh. "Looks worse? Jesus Christ, why haven't you pulled the plug?"

Mom's voice took on the stern tone she used when they were kids and in trouble. "Corey, that's your brother we're talking about."

Corey paced the room while the image of Brian looking like a bloated corpse flooded his mind. What he wanted to do was pick up every piece of furniture and hurl it. He slammed his palm against the wall, and let out an anguished sob. "Did any of you think about what Brian would want? Brian wouldn't want this."

"We're doing everything we can to save your brother's life." The tone of Mom's words now sounded pleading.

Whether she was trying to persuade him or herself, he didn't know. "What kind of life, Mom? You didn't even ask me. I would have told you to let him die."

Why can't they see? Corey threw his arms into the air and shoved his way into the hall. Hahn silently followed him. From the hall, Dana's voice met his ears. "Mom, let him go. Give him some time."

TWENTY-SIX

....

EASTER

The ironic symbolism of Brian lying in a coma with death hovering so close to him now, on Easter Sunday, hit Trish. She'd made sure the boys went to church long enough to be confirmed. Between farming, her work as a prison guard and nurse, and Brian's multiple hospital stays, they'd never managed to be regular in their church attendance. But, Easter had meaning. The decision to go with the Xigris treatment was made on Good Friday, and they'd waited three days, the same amount of time Christ lay dead in a tomb. Like Jesus's mother, Mary, all Trish could do was pray.

As the first rays of sun poured through the stained glass windows of the tiny hospital chapel, Trish, Ray, Dana, Amy, Corey and Hahn joined hands with Pastor Miller, the hospital's white-haired female chaplain. Pots of Easter lilies surrounded the hardwood altar and spilled down toward the empty pews. Pastor Miller bowed her head and spoke in a clear voice, "Heavenly Father, on this Easter Sunday, we ask you to raise up your son Brian. Like you raised up your own son Jesus. Give him strength. Be with this family, and grant them your peace, your strength, and your hope."

The chaplain prayed with them again at Brian's bedside, but this was the moment Trish wanted to remember. Here, in a hospital chapel, they stood together as a family before God, united to face whatever the future might hold for all of them. She made no effort to hide the tears that flowed down her face. Yes, she'd spent decades where she always had to be strong. But sometimes, strength wasn't enough. Sometimes, you had to surrender to something greater than yourself.

Sometimes, you had to have faith.

TWENTY-SEVEN

DYING

Bathed in a dim light, Brian became aware of out-of-focus faces surrounding him. Somehow, they seemed familiar. Comforting. Above him, the beast continued to hover, as soundless screams of fury poured from its drawn mouth.

Something about the monster had changed. Now, along with the heavy drops of blood that dripped onto Brian from the skeletal body, bits of dust crumbled around the edges.

Brian suspected it was dying. What that meant, he didn't know. Would he die along with it? For the first time, instead of simply fear, he experienced a sense of acceptance.

TWENTY-EIGHT

THE RETURN

Trish sat near Brian's bed with Amy on the other side. A doctor she didn't recognize entered with a chart in his hands. He held himself different from most of the caregivers assigned to Brian's case. And there were plenty of caregivers assigned to his case. This guy's posture emitted an air of arrogance. He barely looked at her as he introduced himself. "Dr. Samuels, plastic surgery."

Trish rose from her chair and extended her hand. "I'm Trish Thomas, Brian's mom. This is his girlfriend, Amy."

She might as well have not said anything at all. Dr. Samuels barely nodded in their direction. He donned a pair of gloves and examined Brian's blackened nose and cheeks for all of thirty seconds, if that. He tossed the gloves into the trash and jotted a note in the chart and turned toward the door without so much as a word. Was he kidding? Anger boiled over into Trish's voice. "That's it? Don't you want to see his hands or feet?" She held up Brian's hand. His black fingertips were cold against her palm.

Dr. Samuels turned and leveled his gaze on her. "Mrs. Thomas, your son doesn't need a plastic surgeon. He's going to die. You need to accept it."

The control she had over her anger snapped. She lunged toward him, forcing herself to stop directly in front of his face. She spat the words at him with all of the venom she'd stored since the first phone call telling her of Brian's illness, "Who do you think you are? Get out! Get out of my son's room!"

Somewhere her mind registered Amy's hands pulling her back, her voice trying to soothe her. Dr. Samuels beat a hasty retreat out of the room. Trish didn't care if that man was the best plastic surgeon in the Midwest, even the country, there was no way she'd let him touch her son. "How dare he? How dare he?" Her words came out as pained whispers as she sank into Amy's trembling arms.

* * *

Ray stretched his tall frame to try to get comfortable in a recliner near Brian's bedside. Corey offered to stay with him for a while, and they each tried to find a way to get some sleep. Well, sleep might be too strong a word for it. Between the absolute impossibility of a six foot tall guy finding any way to manipulate himself into any semblance of a comfortable sleeping position in a hospital recliner, the incessant parade of people in and out of the room, and the beeps and clacks of all the machinery attached to Brian, it was fair to say that his unconscious son was the only one getting any real sleep. He glanced over at Corey. His tall slender form shifted slightly in an awkward position, one leg thrown over the armrest of the chair, his head at an odd angle.

At least Brian wasn't on dialysis any more. It made even more noise. They'd managed to get him down to only four IV machines, too. Small steps, but every time the nurses removed another piece of equipment that was helping keep his son alive, Ray had to resist the urge to jump up and down and pump his fists.

Maybe he was being overly optimistic, but he knew his son. Maybe better than anyone else. The knowledge Brian was going to pull through this had never wavered in Ray's heart, even when everyone else seemed to have written him off. He knew the medical staff thought he was deluded. Most of the time, even his own wife did. But somehow he just knew. Brian was going to pull through this. He was going to be okay. And Ray was going to be there when his son opened his eyes for the first time.

Ray's mind flashed back a few years to Easter Sunday, 2000. Brian's first solo flight. He'd stood and watched Brian fly the Cessna 172 around the Yankton airport three times. Brian had crawled out of the airplane so pumped with adrenaline he could barely walk. The smile on Brian's face... it was one of the best memories of Ray's life.

He'd snapped a Polaroid picture of Brian standing in front of the airplane. Ray still had it, at home, wedged into the lid of his toolbox.

A noise from the bed pulled Ray from his thoughts. Brian's eyes fluttered, and his body jerked in the bed. He'd had plenty of random movements over the days he'd been unconscious—enough that the nurses tied his hands to keep all of the lines and wires connected. *Neurological responses*, they called them. *Nothing more than reflexes*, they said. Ray wasn't sure he believed them. If Brian was trying to pull out tubes, it seemed purposeful to him.

The ventilator sputtered as Brian gulped and swallowed. Alarms blared. Corey jumped up from the recliner, nearly pulling it over as he tried to untangle himself from the blanket and chair parts. Ray pushed the call light next to Brian's bed.

Mandy Allison, a pretty young blonde night-nurse, rushed into the room. She fidgeted with the ventilator controls. Corey paced nearby. "What's happening to him?"

Mandy placed her hand on Corey's shoulder. "It's okay, he's just fighting the ventilator."

Ray crept closer and peered down at his son. He reached out and took Brian's hand.

Corey spoke again, "Does that mean he's waking up?"

Mandy pulled a syringe from a locked box near the bed, and injected the contents into Brian's IV tubing. "It might."

Brian's body went limp, his erratic breathing movements replaced by the regular rhythm of the ventilator. His eyelids stopped moving. Ray kept a hold on his son's hand. He looked up at Mandy, confused. "Brian's been unconscious for a week, and now you're sedating him?"

Mandy nodded. "It'll help him. So he won't fight the ventilator."

It might not seem like much to Mandy, but Ray knew this was different. He looked at Corey, whose eyes were still wide with fear. "Go get your mom."

A few hours later, the whole family gathered in Brian's room. A nervous energy seemed to fill them all. Dr. Davis and Dr. Michaelson stood near the elevated head of the bed. Brian's partially open eyes fluttered occasionally. Dr. Davis glanced around at their anxious faces. "Okay, are we ready?"

Ray nodded. *Ready?* He wanted to do it himself. Dr. Davis deflated the balloon on the endotracheal tube with a syringe, unfastened the tape straps that secured it to his son's face, and slid it out of his airway. Brian coughed and gagged. Ray held his breath as he watched and waited for his son to breathe on his own. When Brian drew in a long breath, he noticed almost everyone else in the room did as well. Even Dr. Michaelson.

Dr. Davis smiled. The first time Ray had ever seen the man smile, come to think of it. "Great. Now we wait."

Ray cocked his head. "What are we waiting for?"

Dr. Davis turned toward him. "Since he's breathing on his own, we'll stop the sedatives."

Ray's eyes widened as the realization hit him. "So, he'll wake up?"

The doctor nodded. "That's our hope." He swallowed and stared at the ground a moment before he continued. "I wish I knew what to tell you to expect if and when he does wake up."

Next to him, Corey's jaw clenched. "You're trying to warn us he might be a vegetable."

"It's hard to tell what damage his brain sustained."

Ray broke in, "He's going to be fine." None of them knew Brian like he did. His son was a fighter. He'd show them all.

Corey and Dana exchanged nervous glances. Dana gave a forced smile and nodded. "We'll take it as it comes."

For Ray, the rest of the day took place in a daze. If Brian was quiet, someone rushed to check to see if he was breathing. If he became restless—which happened more frequently, everyone surrounded the bed to try to comfort him. No one seemed to want to leave. Not even long enough to go to the bathroom or eat. Family really wasn't supposed to use the restroom in Brian's room, but if the nurses noticed, they were kind enough not to say anything. Even the medical staff seemed to be spending more time than necessary in his room.

Ray wasn't sure what time it was, or how long it had been since they'd stopped the sedatives and taken Brian off the ventilator. Outside the window, darkness approached, so it had to be evening. Ray's heart filled with hope every time Brian's eyes opened, and then Ray watched him drift back off to wherever his mind was. He wondered if his son was dreaming.

* * *

Brian's eyes opened. He turned his head and looked around. Halos surrounded the lights and made the faces around him blurry. Where was he? He thought he ought to know. A face bent close to him. He struggled to make sense of the features. Mom. *That's my mom. Am I at home? I don't think so. Somewhere else, but where?*

Her lips moved, but Brian couldn't make out what she was saying. Everything around him was at the same time muffled, and all jumbled together into a cacophony of sound. Other faces joined his mother's. Dana. Then his dad. Their mouths moved as well. Why couldn't he remember where he was, or how he got here?

Brian reached up to touch his face. Something was wrong, his hand was wrapped in soft cloth, like a mitten. *People don't wear gloves inside.* Dad pulled his hand away from his face and patted it like you would a child. *But I'm not a little kid anymore. Am I?*

Brian picked the sound of agitated footsteps out of the blur around him. Then words. Corey's strained voice. "He doesn't recognize us, or know who he is."

But he did know. Brian focused on Mom's face and took a deep breath. His voice didn't sound right, like he had a mouthful of cotton, but he forced his lips to make the words. "Hi Mom. I'm still here. It's me, Brian."

Around him, things erupted in a melee of sound and movement. People cried and hugged him, and each other. Brian still had no idea where he was, or what was going on. He stared at the ceiling, where the beast that had been his constant companion usually lurked. All that was there now were ugly white tiles and lights.

TWENTY-NINE

....

YANKTON?

Hal Dipple and Kevin sat next to Brian's bed. Brian's mom had pulled some strings to get them into the intensive care unit. Well, actually, she'd lied and told the nursing staff they were relatives. Personally, Hal didn't think they believed her, but they also didn't argue.

She'd warned them they might not recognize their friend from work, but he hadn't expected anything like this. Brian's face was covered in thick black scabs. Hell, it looked like his nose had rotted on his face. Hal dabbed at the corners of his eyes and cleared his throat. "We thought we'd lost you, Buddy."

Kevin added, "All the guys at Duncan are asking about you."

Brian waved a heavily bandaged hand in the direction of his legs. "My feet won't work."

Hal and Kevin exchanged glances. "We know. Your mom told us." She'd told them his hands and feet looked worse than his face. Much worse.

Brian glanced out the window. "It's too far to walk to Springfield."

Kevin patted Brian's thigh. "Do you know where you are?"

"South Dakota."

Kevin gently corrected him. "You're in Lincoln. You've been sick."

Brian stared at him a moment, his face confused. You could see the wheels turning in his head as he tried to reason through Kevin's words. "There's no Lincoln in South Dakota."

Hal leaned closer to him. "Brian, do you know who I am?

His young protégé nodded. "Yeah, you're my boss."

Good. That was a start. He continued. "And where do you work?"

A look of confusion crossed Brian's face. "Yankton."

That's how it had gone for their entire visit. He'd remember some things, then wander off to this fixation of being in South Dakota. It ripped Hal's heart out. Agitated, he got up and wandered into the hall. The last thing he wanted was for Brian to think he was mad at him.

Once in the waiting room, Hal leaned against the wall and tried to compose himself. Trish, Brian's mother, joined him. He straightened and wiped his eyes again. *For the love of God, don't lose it in front of her.* What the hell was it about this kid that got to him? He guessed it didn't really matter why, but he did know Brian didn't deserve any of the horrible things happening to him.

"It's hard to look at. I know." Trish handed him a cup of water.

Hal reached out and took it, more out of reflex than a desire for something to drink. "I had no idea it would be this bad." He stared at the pattern on the carpet covering the waiting room floor for a moment. "Do they think he'll ever be –well, the same?"

Trish sighed and slumped against the wall. "Who knows? He recognizes us, so that's a start. One thing at a time, right?" A sad smile crossed her face.

THIRTY

BURN UNIT

Brian reflexively took in several deep breaths while Doctor Davis moved the stethoscope around his chest and listened, both on the front and again on the back. Across the room, his parents watched with anxious expressions. When he finished, Dr. Davis pulled the earpieces from his ears, slung the stethoscope around his neck, and smiled. "Looks like we need to get you set up with some new digs."

Brian's parents hugged and beamed. *What are they so excited for?* He'd seen his hands and feet when the nurses changed the dressings. Somehow, he doubted very much they were going to send him home, and that was the only kind of new digs he was really interested in."You kicking me out?"

The doctor touched his bandaged hand. "Yup. We're going to send you across town to get fixed up."

Brian had known this day would come sooner or later. Even though he wasn't looking forward to another uncertain future, doing something was better than being stuck in a bed doing nothing.

* * *

Apparently, he'd be stuck in a bed doing nothing for at least a few more hours. It took a seemingly endless parade of medical personnel to arrange the transfer to the St. Elizabeth Burn Center across town.

Brian asked why he was being sent there. He wasn't burned, his skin looked more, well, dead. The nurses explained the burn specialists were also the best prepared to deal with his type of wounds. In the meantime, there were forms to sign, even calls to his insurance company for authorization before they could actually move him. Finally, two emergency medical technicians rolled a narrow ambulance cot into his room.

It took more time to move him to the gurney. The attendants had to wrangle his remaining lines and tubes into place. Then there were a bunch more forms to fill out before Mom made a final check of his room to make sure they hadn't forgotten anything.

Finally, the entourage made it into the hall. As they approached the nurses' station, it looked like every nurse who'd taken care of him had shown up to see him off. Several of the staff bent to give Brian hugs as they wheeled past.

The brief moments outside before they loaded him into the back of the ambulance were a welcome reprise. A crisp breeze and the scent of fresh spring air brushed his face. Brian had gotten used to the antiseptic smells of the hospital. It was to the point where he didn't even notice it. All too soon, the attendants jostled his cot into the back of the waiting ambulance and secured it for the trip.

The drive was too short. Brian tried to look out the narrow back window to catch a glimpse of the outside. The world continued to turn without him, but even with the head of the cot elevated, it was hard to see much at all.

Once they arrived at the emergency entrance at St. Elizabeth Community Medical Center, the process reversed. Unstrap the gurney, bounce around as the attendants lowered the cot to the ground, a few precious breaths of fresh air, then back inside.

A whole new series of antiseptic aromas flooded Brian's senses. After a brief wait while the receptionist talked to his attendants and his parents joined them, they piled into a back elevator to head up to the Burn Unit.

One thing Brian did like was having a private room. It wasn't nearly as noisy, which might mean he could sleep more than five minutes at a time.

Brian turned his head from an episode of South Park when his door opened. Two scrub-clad techs pushed in a stainless-steel table covered with a clear plastic bag of some sort. A tall, bearded African-American guy who had to be around his age nodded. "I'm Shimiah. Shimiah Brown. This is Amber." He gestured to the young blonde woman beside him. "We're going to get you cleaned up."

Brian frowned. "Not looking forward to this." He'd heard plenty of horror stories about burn treatment, even watched comedian Richard Pryor talk about the pain he'd endured after he was burned.

Amber chuckled. "Probably not, but I hear the morphine is nice."

At least she was honest. He'd give her that much.

They helped him slide onto the waiting table. Brian flinched and gave an involuntary shiver as his bare backside hit the cold surface. "Fuck, did you pull this thing out of a freezer?"

Shimiah laughed and threw a blanket over him.

The tub room was right down the hall from his room, right on the burn unit itself. Handy. It looked like an operating room, with a big drain in the middle of the floor. A nurse waited in the corner, with a handful of syringes in her hand. A small table covered with a green towel and an array of surgical instruments stood nearby. Brian didn't like the look of those sharp implements at all.

Sound echoed as Shimiah and Amber helped Brian out of his gown. Shimiah placed a towel over his groin. The pair unwound and cut off the dressings covering the black oozing blisters on his arms and legs. His fingers and toes looked black and shriveled. He tried to move them, but it was like they were asleep and wouldn't obey his commands.

Shimiah grabbed a hose hanging from the ceiling and a surgical scrub sponge from one of the tables. "Let's get you smelling good before the doctor gets here."

He turned the hose on and sprayed Brian's arm with a pulsating stream of warm water. A blister on his upper arm broke open and the skin sloughed away to reveal open raw tissue beneath. Brian let out a breath he hadn't known he was holding. "That's not so bad."

Shimiah made a non-committal grunt. He raised the scrub brush. "If I were you, I'd hold that thought for a while."

The tech whistled as he scrubbed the sponge across Brian's exposed raw skin. Fire shot up his arm like a jolt of electricity. Whatever sound came out of his mouth, it must have been pretty bad, because it brought the silent nurse with a syringe to his bed-side. A few moments later, Brian drifted off into a semblance of twilight to the sound of running water as a sense of warmth and calm overtook him.

Brian came to with his wet head propped up on a roll of cloth. More dry towels covered his body. A red glare emitted from a heat lamp directly above him. Fortunately, the afterglow of the pain medicine was still with him, too.

A tall Asian doctor in scrubs, gloves, and a face mask approached the table. Shimiah nodded at him. "He's ready for you, Dr. Hao."

The burn doctor leaned over the table and met Brian's gaze. "Okay, Brian, Let's see what we are dealing with."

He removed the towel covering Brian's right hand and arm. The nurse pushed the tray with surgical instruments closer to him. He picked up a scalpel. Brian's eyes widened as Dr. Hao turned his blackened hand over and prodded the pads of his fingertips with the sharp tip. He eyed the nurse, hoping she had more pain medicine nearby.

"Does this hurt?" The doctor raised his eyes to Brian.

Well, huh. "I don't feel a thing."

Brian noticed Shimiah's brow furrowed as he and Dr. Hao exchanged glances. The doctor continued to prod at the black tissue. As he neared Brian's wrist, a drop of blood welled from the puncture site. Brian sucked in a deep breath. "Ow! I felt that one."

Dr. Hao nodded and moved to his other side. He removed the towel from Brian's left arm and repeated the process, then moved down to his feet.

When the doctor finished poking and prodding, Shimiah and Amber covered his open wounds with a thick white cream and cocoon-like dressings.

Back in his room, Brian rested with his head raised. His parents, brothers, and Amy sat with him as they waited for Dr. Hao's verdict. The burn doctor carried Brian's chart as he pulled a chair up to the bedside. His family exchanged nervous glances. Amy held Brian's bandaged hand tight in her grip.

Dr. Hao didn't mince any words. "He has a lot of dead tissue. We'll have to amputate."

Mom broke the stunned silence following his announcement. "Amputate how much?"

Dr. Hao cleared his throat. "Most likely both legs below the knee, and both hands."

The words rang in Brian's ears. Deep inside, he'd already guessed this might happen, but now the words echoed with solemn finality. He was only vaguely aware of Amy's tears, or his dad's face buried in his hands. Everyone seemed to be staring at him with pained expressions. Sorrow? Regret? Pity? Well, what choice did he have? He steeled himself and uttered a single word, his voice hollow. "When?"

"Tomorrow morning. The surgery will likely take all day." Dr. Hao stood and headed to the door. Before he disappeared into the hall, he turned briefly and gave Brian a pointed look. "I am sorry."

* * *

Brian looked at the pills in the tiny paper cup. "What are these?"

His nurse smiled at him. "One for pain, and something to help you sleep."

He gave her a questioning look. He really wasn't in that much pain. It was more of a dull ache, really. And he wasn't sure he needed a sleeping pill.

She reached out and touched his arm. "It will help you to take your mind off tomorrow."

Okay, that made sense. Brian hadn't been able to stop thinking about the looming surgery since Dr. Hao's words.

Amputate.

He was twenty five years old, for Christ's sake. Grandpa was missing part of his left hand, so Brian knew it was possible to live as an amputee. But how would he manage without any hands or feet? Fear gripped him. He tipped his head back and chased the pills with a swig of water.

He woke later to a dim room, lit by the soft green glow of the four IV pumps standing guard at his bedside. They clicked and chugged in discordant harmony. Brian squirmed in the bed, trying to find a comfortable position. He sat up and eyed the empty recliner beside him.

Brian pulled himself up using his bedside table to steady himself. Just a couple of steps to the chair. He could do it, no problem. He shuffled his feet in the direction of the waiting recliner. The table skated across the room, and he landed on the floor in a tangle of IV tubing and sheets.

Shimiah ran into the room. He scooped Brian up in a giant bear-hug and deposited him onto the side of the bed. "Hey, where do you think you're going?"

He wasn't sure, but the idea of running away sounded pretty damned good about right now. Pretend everything was a giant nightmare, and he'd wake up and it would disappear, just like the monster he'd seen in the intensive care unit. Brian glanced at the recliner. "The chair?"

Shimiah shook his head. His voice was soft and quiet. "Buddy, your feet are dead. You will be too, if we don't fix you up."

Brian scowled and stared at the wall. He knew that. Somehow, he'd hoped for a few precious moments to forget.

Shimiah lifted Brian's legs into the bed. "Well, you're going to get hurt trying to walk, so stay put. Okay?"

* * *

Early the next morning, more nurses with nameless faces loaded him up onto another gurney. Brian was really learning to hate those damned things. They wheeled him into a brightly lit operating room downstairs. Several gowned and masked nurses and scrub techs readied instrument trays as others slid him onto the table.

Some of them introduced themselves, but most went about their business like he didn't exist. Cold, sterile, and impersonal. Well, he supposed they were used to dealing with people who were asleep and didn't care one way or another. Above him, hoses hung from the ceiling and a huge light glared into his eyes.

Brian turned his head and stared at the trays of sharp surgical instruments. In the middle was a circular bone saw. He took a deep breath and held it as he squeezed his eyes shut. A few tears made their way onto his cheeks. He swallowed hard.

This was it.

There was no going back. An image from a horror movie flashed through his mind. Him with nothing but stumps where his arms and legs had been, and gruesome lines of bloody sutures.

Only this wasn't a horror movie, or a nightmare.

It was much worse.

Near his head, the anesthesiologist, patted his arm. "I'm Doctor Carver. I'll be taking care of you today, making sure you have a nice nap. I'm going to give you something to relax, okay?"

Brian took in a deep breath and nodded.

The doctor squirted the contents of a syringe into his IV tubing. He grabbed a mask from a nearby cart and placed it over Brian's face. "Just breathe normally. Some people dream. Think of a happy place."

The sounds and colors around him in the room blurred to white.

THIRTY-ONE

AMPUTATED

Brian's eyes opened in his dimly lit room. He glanced down at his hands. They were wrapped in huge bandages. So were his legs. It was impossible to tell through all of the padding how much of his body they'd had to cut off. He took a deep breath. At least his nightmares of stubs nearly to his thighs and shoulders wasn't true.

Then a wave of pain struck him. Brian thrashed in the bed, and even though he tried to stop the sounds from coming out, screamed.

Shimiah and Chelsea, one of his favorite nurses, ran into the room.

"Fuck, it hurts! Where's Mom and Amy? Where is everybody?" Brian's eyes searched through the darkness for a familiar face.

Tears blurred his vision. He tried to dry them with his bandaged hands but it didn't help. Were there still hands under the bandages?

Chelsea dashed back out the door while Shimiah rubbed his shoulder. "It's late." He shook his head. "They had a hard time after seeing pictures of the surgery. They left."

Brian continued to thrash and kick his legs. They hurt so bad. The movement might not help stop the pain, but he couldn't control it. Frustration boiled over inside him. "I'm laying here hacked up like a piece of meat, and *they're* having a hard time?"

Chelsea rushed back into the room with a syringe and some ice bags. She injected the medicine into his IV tubing. She and Shimiah elevated Brian's legs and applied the ice bags. In a few moments, he drifted back into a painful daze.

Sunlight now streamed through the window. Brian really didn't know what time it was, though. Everything revolved around the waves of pain between pain shots. He squirmed in his bed.

Mom fumed as she paced nearby, watching as Chelsea injected medicine into his IV tubing. "What idiot thought self-administered pain medicine was a good idea?"

Chelsea gave her an understanding glance. "Anesthesia thought he would be more comfortable if he could control it himself."

Mom stomped over to his bedside and grabbed a button that resembled a nurse call light. Her voice rose. "You need fingers to push the button!"

* * *

Brian worried how he'd react the first time he saw the stumps on his hand and feet. But as Dr. Hao unwound the gauze on his right stump, he found himself morbidly fascinated and detached by what remained of his arm. It reminded him of a dissection lab in biology, with all the exposed muscle and tissue. Somewhere along the line, he'd switched to autopilot mode. It made things a lot easier to cope.

Between nearly daily trips to the operating room with more anesthesia, extensive tub room sessions where Dr. Hao pared dead skin from his remaining left hand and pain medications, the following days passed in a drug-induced haze.

Today, they focused on what used to be his right hand. Raw open skin covered the lower half of his arm, down to the stump, which was where his wrist used to be. Brian watched them work with almost a detached sense of wonder. It was as if the thing at the end of his arm wasn't really attached to him, but he couldn't tear his attention away from his body being remodeled.

In his mind, when he thought about moving his fingers, it seemed like they moved, even though the only thing he noticed was a slight ripple in the muscles on his lower arm. Dr. Hao said that was a good thing, those muscles would control a prosthetic arm when he healed enough to get fitted for one. So, Brian occupied his spare time flexing fingers that were probably embedded in wax in a pathologist's office. Maybe they'd already incinerated his discarded body parts. He hadn't really asked what happened to them, although he had considered seeing if he could keep them in a jar and take them home. He'd earned the right, after all. Hadn't he?

The pain from his hand was bad, but nothing like his feet. Or, what remained of his feet. The nurses located a soft round button for him to use for the patient controlled anesthesia. The idea made sense. Whenever he hurt, he pushed the button, and a small dose of medication released from a machine directly into his bloodstream through his IV tubing. But in reality, it wasn't always so smooth. The stupid button got lost in his bed. Or he'd be trying to sleep, and the pain would get so bad before it woke him up that he'd spend the next couple hours trying to get the medicine to take it away. His legs always seemed to want to move in the bed, trying to find a comfortable position where none existed.

His feet now ended just a little past his ankle. The skin didn't even cover the muscles and black tissue. Suction devices called wound vacs covered the open areas to help pull things together until they could skin-graft over the stumps. Brian thought everything he'd been through with his ITP had made him pretty tough where it came to pain, but the first time Shimiah changed the suction dressings on his foot stumps, he thought he might actually pass out.

"I'm sorry, Buddy. I know it hurts." Shimiah kept up a quiet stream of conversation, even though Brian struggled and screamed through the worst of it. "One down one to go. Tell me when you're ready."

Brian looked at the ceiling and nodded. Chelsea held his leg down as Shimiah went to work.

His words gave Brian something to hang on to, even though it was the worst thing he'd ever experienced. He closed his eyes and tried to focus on the sound of Shimiah's voice, the cadence to his speech, even when the fire in his feet drowned out the actual words.

Finally, Shimiah stood up and took in a deep breath. "Hard part is over today, Bud."

Brian bent his leg and looked at his foot. A clear plastic film held a black sponge against what remained. A few drops of dark red blood drained in the tubing attached to the vacuum pump. A sense of overwhelming helplessness and despair overtook him.

THIRTY-TWO

....

WHAT?

The day after his third trip to the operating room, Brian opened his eyes as a loud ringing filled his ears. He covered them with his bandaged hands. The sound continued to blast through his head. Shimiah pushed in the gurney to take him to the tub room. The tech's lips moved, but he couldn't hear his voice over the ringing. It wasn't any alarm he'd ever heard before. *Fire?* Why wasn't Shimiah shutting it off? Brian yelled to make himself heard over the sound. "Dude, what's that buzzing? Turn it off, I can't hear you."

Shimiah gave him a puzzled look. He moved closer to Brian's bed and his lips moved again.

Brian heard nothing except the constant ringing.

Shimiah left, and Chelsea came in with an old-fashioned tuning fork. She slapped it in her hands and held it next to his ears.

Nothing.

She slapped it again, and placed the end on the bone behind his ear. *How odd?* He could feel the fork vibrate, but he couldn't hear it. Maybe a tiny bit on his left, but absolutely nothing on the right.

A few hours later, a guy in a dress shirt and slacks came in with a cart. His name tag said he was Craig. The middle aged guy placed a set of headphones over Brian's ears. Craig adjusted some knobs on the portable testing equipment. He then wrote on a piece of paper for Brian to point to his ear if he heard anything on that side.

Brian concentrated on trying to pick out sounds through the constant ringing. Occasionally, he'd pick out the electronic tone in different pitches, but always on his left side. He tried watching Craig's face to see how he was doing, but this guy could be a professional poker player for all his face gave away.

After a few minutes, Craig gave him a different set of headphones, this time attached to a small box about the size of an old-school walkman. He adjusted the dials then smiled. "Okay, Brian, can you hear me?"

Brian nodded. "A little bit."

Craig turned the dial on the box again. "Better?"

It was an improvement, but still not good. "I'm not hearing anything on the right but ringing."

The audiologist nodded. "Yeah, I know. We'll get you fitted for a real hearing aid for your left ear."

Hearing aid? Brian scowled. "This gonna be permanent?"

Craig patted his arm. He even let the poker face he'd used during his hearing test drop enough to show a hint of sadness. "Most likely."

Brian shook his head and snorted. Of course it was going to be permanent. Just like his feet and hands. Why would he think anything else?

* * *

Shimiah carried a dinner tray to Brian's bedside. He sat it down and pushed the button to raise Brian's head. "Doc says you can try exercising your stomach. How about some food?"

Brian tried to remember the last thing he ate. Since he'd been sick, the only nutrition he'd been allowed went through either a feeding tube, or his IV. Surprisingly enough, he hadn't missed eating nearly as much as he would have guessed. Between the surgeries and constant trips to the tub room, he'd spent most of his time being half-awake on pain medicine anyway. On the other hand... "A cheeseburger sounds great."

Shimiah lifted the lid on the tray to reveal some orange Jello cubes, broth, a couple packets of crackers, and some juice. "Well, the Jello doesn't look too bad. If this goes okay, we'll work on getting you some real food."

Brian fumbled with the padded spoon Shimiah placed in his left hand. *If this goes okay?* That didn't make much sense to him at all. You eat. End of story, right? Well, that's what he thought until a few hours later when the first wave of nausea hit him. Brian held a basin and vomited a stream of liquefied Jello and broth. He laid his head against the pillow and gasped.

The next afternoon, Shimiah brought in another tray.

More Jello.

"Great. I'll get to puke green today."

Shimiah patted his shoulder. "Your stomach isn't used to food. It might take a while to re-train it."

Brian poked his spoon at the cubes in the dish. It was a good thing he hadn't started out trying to eat a cheeseburger. With all the puking, he was rapidly developing an aversion to Jello, and the last thing he wanted to do was hate something he enjoyed as much as he did burgers.

THIRTY-THREE

··

GRAFTS

Dr. Hao brought the instrument used to harvest the skin they'd need to begin grafting his hand and stumps to show Brian. It reminded him of a hand planer from high school woodworking class. Or a carrot peeler. The doctor wouldn't even fathom a guess when Brian tried to pin him down on how many more surgeries he'd be forced to endure for the skin grafting. And somehow the whole prospect of having skin peeled from his thighs and stapled to other parts of his body sounded painful. It was beginning to make sense why they'd sent him to a burn unit.

Painful didn't begin to describe it. Not quite the same as the agony he'd been through in the immediate aftermath of the amputations, but this was a gnawing ache that never let up. Like the worst rug burn ever, but all over his thighs. Giant scabs formed over the donor sites, and the staples tugged every time he tried to move the areas where he had new grafts.

Brian and Mom watched the Fourth of July fireworks display from his hospital window. She even got permission for him to try a little bit of ice cream to celebrate the holiday, even though cele-

161

brating was the last thing on his mind. "You're getting so skinny. Look at your face. You hardly look like my Brian anymore."

He wasn't sure what *her Brian*, meant. The Brian he'd been before didn't exist. The Brian he'd been in the Intensive Care Unit? *What?* He didn't care enough to ask. Instead, he just nodded and shoveled a couple of bites of ice cream into his mouth to pacify her. Not that it would matter, he'd throw it up later tonight, like he did everything else he tried to eat. Or it would give him bloody diarrhea. If he was really lucky, both. Wasn't worth the effort most of the time.

* * *

Brian turned his head as something metal clattered from the door to his room. Shimiah pushed a wheelchair next to his bed. Mom followed close behind him. The burn tech stroked his beard as his intense gaze leveled on Brian. "I'm thinking a change of scenery might be good."

Change of scenery as in what? Tub room? Operating room? Recovery room? Thanks, but no thanks.

But Shimiah wasn't taking no for an answer. Before Brian could even protest, he'd been loaded into the wheelchair. Shimiah pushed, and Mom took the rear, pushing his IV pump behind them down the hallway. As the elevator doors closed behind them, Brian warily eyed the two. "Where are we going?"

Mom grinned. "It's a surprise."

Brian snorted. "My surprises end up being things like, 'Hey, you don't have any feet,' or, 'didn't need that hearing, did you?'"

He noticed Shimiah and Mom exchanging concerned glances. Yeah, he was being cynical. He'd earned the right. If they didn't like it, tough. Shimiah pushed him out of the elevator into a small patio adjoining the cafeteria. He locked the wheels on the chair near a glass-topped table. The scent of summer flowers in hanging baskets nearby flooded Brian's senses as a gentle breeze ruffled his hair.

Shimiah nodded. "Just call when you're ready to go back up." He glanced up at the clear afternoon sky. "Keep him under the umbrella. I know he's in the burn unit, but we don't need any sunburns."

Brian closed his eyes and took in a few deep breaths. Mom slid into a seat at the table beside him and patted his arm. "Nice, isn't it?"

"They even let prison inmates outside once a day." Brian tried not to notice her flinch at his words. He tugged at the headphones that had been his constant companion since he'd lost his hearing.

Why it was taking so long to get a hearing aid made for him, he'd never know. Let those idiot executives in a hearing aid company have to deal with awkward ineffective headphones to hear anything at all, and he'd bet they could figure out how to decrease the turnaround time for ear molds.

"Hey, Mom, can you stop by my apartment and grab my good earbud headphones? These suck."

Mom shifted in her seat and stared at the ground. "Sweetheart, we moved your stuff to Amy's house a while back."

Brian stiffened. *What?* His voice raised. "Why the hell did you do that?"

She reached out for him, her expression pained, her eyes begging him to understand. "You can't think you'll be able to live by yourself after you're discharged."

Brian pulled away from her. "Damn it, Mom. Maybe I don't want to live with Amy. Did you ever think about that?"

"She's good for you, Brian. She's hung in there through all of this."

Brian threw his headset on the table using his elbows. It wasn't like he didn't like Amy, but they were just dating. Nothing forever-serious. Yes, she'd been hinting about making things more...permanent. And he'd been doing a damn good job of avoiding the subject. Just like two women to get together and force him into a decision he didn't want to make. "Take me back to my cell."

Mom picked the headphones up and placed them back on his head. She waited until he looked at her before speaking. "Brian–"

"What? Isn't it true? My sentence is to live the rest of my life..." he threw his arms into the air, "...stuck in this damn body. I swear, I've been cursed my entire life." He slumped back against the wheelchair.

"We've done the best we knew how to do, Honey."

"I wanted to die in that fucking operating room when they cut off my hand. My feet. My life." Brian knew his words were hurting her, but he couldn't help it. "They brought me a bunch of paperwork from Social Security. How sad is it? I can't even sign disability papers." He held up the bandaged stump that used to be his right hand.

They sat there in silence. For how long, he wasn't sure. What more was there to say? The breeze brushing against him any other time would be welcome. Today, it tasted as flat and bland as the food the cafeteria served him. It would probably find a way to come back and hurt him later anyway, just like everything he ate, too.

THIRTY-FOUR

....

TATE

It didn't take long for Brian to start looking forward to going outside to sit on the patio, though. Even though it only took a few days before it became little more than another part of the monotonous routine of life in the burn unit. Even so, for a few precious minutes, he gazed at the clouds and remembered his old life when he soared among them. Some days, it was a comfort. Others, a mocking reminder of how much he'd lost.

From his elevated bed, Brian fumbled with a padded spoon as he tried to scoop a bite of Jello into his mouth. On the screen of the television across the room, the image of a crashed small plane caught his attention. He pushed the control to increase the volume. The words, "Breaking News from Sioux Falls, South Dakota," scrolled across the bottom of the screen. He put down the spoon and leaned forward as the camera panned in to where a reporter stood near the wreckage. "FAA authorities say the pilot, Flight Instructor Tate Baloun, died when his homebuilt airplane crashed shortly after takeoff this morning. Early reports are the small plane lost engine power..."

Brian watched the screen, his mouth agape. *Tate?*

No way.

He wiped his eyes with his bandaged arm, then shoved his bedside table. It collided with the wall. His water pitcher and glass crashed to the floor, along with the remnants of his Jello.

Shimiah rushed in. His shrewd gaze took in the mess and Brian's expression. "You okay, buddy?"

"It's not fair."

Shimiah cleaned up the mess and answered, his voice calm and soothing. "Never is."

Brian swatted at his tears. "How fucked up is this? I find out my flight instructor, someone I was proud to call a friend, dies in a plane crash, and all I can think is that he's a lucky bastard."

Shimiah grabbed the office chair from the nearby computer desk. He pulled it over next to Brian's bed and sat, straddling the chair. He leaned on the backrest and surveyed Brian. "Talk to me."

"What?"

"You're right. You got fucked. But, you ain't the only one. I see it every day in here."

Brian snorted. "Thanks a bunch, Shimiah. Way to cheer me up."

He shook his head. "You've got it all wrong, Buddy. It's not about cheering you up, it's about waking you up."

Yeah, right. "Dude, I was in a coma for a week. That and after all the surgeries, I think I know about waking up."

"You cover pretty well with sarcasm." Shimiah paused and stroked his beard a moment. "You ever think about suicide?"

Brian flinched. "Every day." He stared out the window, wondering why he was telling Shimiah this. Why was he was telling anyone about the darkness in the back of his mind? Not that it mattered. "I can't tie a sheet in a knot to hang myself. I'd try starving, but I'm on IV nutrition, so short of begging one of you guys to put a bullet in my head, I'm screwed."

His eyes met Shimiah's dark brown ones. Brian wasn't sure what he expected to find reflected in them. Disappointment, anger, fear? Instead he saw nothing but acceptance. The tech nodded.

Brian continued, "I won't ever ride my motorcycle or fly. I can't even fucking walk. Hell, I need help to wipe my own ass. I'm an airplane mechanic. What am I supposed to do now?"

Shimiah placed a hand on his arm. "I'm not going to give you any of that 'God never gives us more than we can handle' bullshit." He clapped Brian on the shoulder. "But I do know that to figure it out, you're going to need to stop focusing on what you've lost, and start looking at what you have."

THIRTY-FIVE

JESSIE

Brian and Amy sat beside an umbrella-covered table in the early August afternoon. It was a weekend, and his folks were supposed to be coming to see him. His long hospital stay made things hard for Dad. Farming was in full swing, so he was already having to balance trips to Lincoln to see him with chores.

Today, Dad carried Mom's oversized purse to the table. He grabbed a seat near Brian, but continued to hold her purse on his lap. He jostled the bag a few times, until a small black and white puppy poked its head out.

Brian looked from the puppy to his dad, confused. "You can't bring a dog in here! Why'd you buy another dog, anyway?"

Dad laughed and pulled the puppy out of the purse. He plopped it into Brian's lap. "We didn't buy us another dog, we bought you a dog."

Oh, that made perfect sense. "I can't take care of a puppy. Besides, my apartment doesn't allow pets." Brian thought about his words, and scowled. "Never mind, I don't have an apartment."

Amy reached over and petted the puppy. It licked her out-stretched hand and gave an excited yip. "I'll help take care of her, Honey. What do you want to name her?"

The little dog lifted her head and licked Brian's cheek. She smelled like puppy breath, all fresh and new. Dad beamed at him from across the table. "I thought maybe Fifi."

Brian gave a reluctant chuckle. "Yeah right. Fifi? No." It didn't even sound right coming out of a guy's mouth. He tried to imagine going to the door and calling, "Here, Fifi, here, FiFi."

Nope. Not happening.

"Well, come up with something. She's your dog. We thought you'd like her."

Brian ruffled the puppy's head with his bandaged hand and thought a minute. An old Rick Springfield song popped into his head. "How about Jessie? It's more dignified."

Amy smiled and kissed him. "Jessie it is."

* * *

After his folks and Amy left, taking the little furball with them, Chelsea brought Brian his pills. He eyed them in the little paper soufflé cup. Pills that were supposed to help him keep the food in his stomach. Not that they seemed to be helping with that very much. He shook the cup a bit. "What's the little blue one? I don't recognize it."

Chelsea stammered as her face flushed a brilliant red. She needed to take some lessons from Craig the audiologist if she ever wanted to learn how to play poker. Brian raised an eyebrow. "Okay, out with it."

"All right, it's an antidepressant. Your mom and the doctor thought that it might help with the..."

Brian cut her off. "Antidepressants? What am I, some nut-case now?"

The nurse put her hands up as if to fend off his accusations. "No one thinks that. But, you've been through so much."

He threw the cup. The pills bounced out and scattered across the floor. "Stop drugging me behind my back."

Brian stared out the window a few moments. It wasn't her fault. She was just following orders. But the fact that people he'd trusted were whispering about him... They'd already gotten rid of his apartment without asking him, so why would anyone think to ask him what he thought about anything? What else was going on that he didn't know about?

He leveled his gaze to Chelsea's frightened face. "I want to look at all the drugs I'm taking."

"I'll have to ask the doctor for permission for you to look at your chart..."

He cut her off again. "Fine. You tell him I have to live in this body, and I'm going to damn well decide what goes into it."

Brian folded his arms and stared at her. She ducked her head and beat a hasty retreat. Most likely to make a phone call to the doctor. Good. He'd had more than enough of other people controlling his life. He was a grown man, and it was high time people started treating him like it.

All of them.

Mom included.

Brian pulled a wheelchair close to his bed. He lifted himself up and heaved himself into the seat. Amy walked into the room as he was mid-air. She rushed to his bedside. "Wait a minute. Let me help you. Why didn't you call someone?" She tried to take his arm.

And it definitely included Amy. Brian shoved her away. "I don't want your help. If I do, I'll ask for it. Okay?"

Her voice took on that patronizing tone you use for little kids and old people. "But you'll fall, Honey."

And? He glared at her. "Yeah, and I'm gonna have to figure it out on my own sometime."

Amy folded her arms across her chest. She wasn't patronizing him anymore, now she was pissed. "What the hell has gotten into you today?"

Fine. He could play that game, too. "Everybody thinks I am going to sit back and let you figure out the rest of my life for me. You, Mom, the doctors." Brian glared at her and wheeled himself to the door. "Not anymore. I'm calling the shots. You don't like it, you don't have to hang around and watch."

Brian ended up back out on the deserted patio. A hint of dusk clouded the sky overhead. He sat alone at a table in the wheelchair. With the headphones on, he could just pick out the hum of traffic on 70th Street. This time of year, there should be a drone of cicadas in the background, but even using his imagination, he couldn't make it out. Maybe he'd never hear them again.

Shimiah approached, his arm full with a tray containing a couple cheeseburgers, fries, and sodas. He sat at Brian's table and took a bite of cheeseburger.

Brian glared at him. "I suppose they sent you to talk some sense into me."

The burly tech leaned back and chewed his food. "Nope. I'm on my lunch break."

Brian did a double-take as the smell made his mouth water. "Well, you're an asshole. Cheeseburgers? You know what kind of crap they serve me up there."

Shimiah grinned and shoved the tray closer to Brian. "Yup. That's why I got two."

Pissed or not, Brian grabbed a burger and took a bite. The sharp tang of ketchup and pickles mingled with cheese hit his tongue. "Fuck, that's good. Are you gonna get in trouble for letting me eat this?" He swallowed the bite and washed it down with a deep draught of Mountain Dew from the cup Shimiah pointed toward.

"Like I said, I'm on my lunch break."

The two men ate in silence for a few moments. Then Shimiah gave him a long stare and nodded, waving his half-eaten burger in Brian's direction. "You're going to be all right, Thomas. You're going to be all right."

THIRTY-SIX

....

MADONNA

Things started happening quickly, once Brian decided to rejoin his life. Dr. Hao informed him his grafts were healing well, and it was time to get on with the serious business of rehabilitation. In other words, learning how to adjust to life outside a hospital and without a staff of nurses and technicians to help him.

He spent days talking to social workers, admissions workers, and insurance adjustors while they arranged for a bed for him at the Madonna Rehabilitation Hospital. He'd cringed a bit when he noticed the title included the word, *hospital,* but he'd quickly been assured it would be nothing like what he'd experienced so far. In fact, it might be closer to Boot Camp than a hospital.

Brian sat in a wheelchair in a T-shirt and sweat pants. Regular clothes, instead of those horrible hospital gowns. That was a real start. He couldn't keep the grin off his face as Mom wheeled him from his burn unit room into the hall.

Much like when he'd been transferred from the Intensive Care Unit at Lincoln General/Bryan West to St. Elizabeth's, it seemed like the whole unit had shown up to see him off. Dr. Hao rose from the Nurses' Station desk as they approached, along with Shimiah, Amber, and Chelsea. Oddly enough, Brian found himself choking back a huge lump in his throat. "The Brian Thomas Room is officially vacant."

Dr. Hao shook his hand, a bit awkward, since Brian had to shake with his left hand now, but he managed. The doctor spoke. "They'll take good care of you at Madonna."

Brian nodded. "I don't plan on being there long enough to find out."

Shimiah laughed, a deep baritone rumble. "Yeah, well, they won't let you lay around all day there. Rehab is work." He clapped Brian on the back and bent to hug him. His voice sounded low, next to Brian's good ear, where a hearing aid now replaced the awkward headphones. "You stay cool. Don't make me come over there and give you an ass-kicking."

Brian hugged him in return and replied just loud enough for Shimiah to hear, "Next time, it'll take more than a cheeseburger. At least a good juicy steak."

Amber and Chelsea hugged him. The lump in Brian's throat now threatened to choke him. He caught Mom's eye and nodded. She wheeled him toward the exit.

Downstairs, he was met by the driver from Madonna, an older guy who helped Brian transfer into a different wheelchair, this one with the Madonna name inked on the back, instead of St. Elizabeth's. Outside, the driver used a lift to raise the wheelchair with Brian in it into the back of a small bus-like transport van.

Unlike the ride to St. Elizabeth's, this time Brian got to appreciate the view a bit from the van's windows. Colors swirled by as they drove past Holmes Lake. He'd been stuck inside since before

Easter. Missed all of spring and summer. Now the heat of summer had started to give way to cooler nights. Soon the leaves would be in that spectacular stage of turning. Bright reds and oranges. He'd never been one to spend a lot of time thinking about things like leaves turning. Funny how little things like color made such a difference in life.

The bus pulled up to the Madonna campus. A large glass pyramid supported on brick pillars covered the entrance to the building. The surrounding grounds were spacious, green, and well-tended.

The driver repeated the loading process in reverse to lower Brian in his wheelchair to the ground. Mom climbed out of the side door and wheeled him to the entrance. Inside, they passed by a large open lounge area. A little blonde girl who couldn't have been more than five years old sat in a miniature wheelchair next to a large aquarium filled with brightly colored fish. He wondered what had happened to her.

A couple of men looked up from a card game with passing interest as they wheeled past. *They probably wonder what happened to me, too.* Brian supposed he would have to get used to people staring at him. He hadn't even considered that.

On the other side of the lounge, a young guy–had to be about his age–sat in front of a large-screen television. A huge metal cage surrounded his head and back. Screws held it to his scalp near his temples. Halo traction, he'd heard of them before. Must have broken his neck. The social workers had told him Madonna had one of the best head and neck injury recovery programs in the region, if not the country.

Mom pushed his wheelchair into a large corner room. "You're spoiled, you know it? You got your private room."

Her smile belied her words. But Brian had pushed pretty hard to get a private room. He'd spent months with people coming and going all the time. A bit of privacy was something he looked forward to.

He surveyed the room. Hardwood floors, tall ceiling, and a window overlooking a landscaped portion of the campus. Not bad. Not bad at all. "I'm too much of an asshole to room with anyone."

Mom laughed and swatted him upside the head. Already things seemed more *normal.*

A short blonde woman in dark blue scrubs and athletic shoes knocked on his door and walked into his room. "I'm Renee, your primary care nurse. Don't get too comfortable. You've got a shopping trip in half an hour."

Well, huh. "What for?" He'd never been one to enjoy shopping.

She smiled. "To pick out your wheelchair." She raised a warning finger in his direction. "But don't get excited about using it much. You'll be too busy learning how to walk."

* * *

True to her words, a half hour later, Brian sat on a low physical therapy table in a spacious room. Nearby were a pair of walking assist bars. Renee pressed a wooden yardstick against his back and wrote measurements on his chart.

A slender guy in a bright red wheelchair propelled himself toward them with arms that looked like he lifted weights. A catalog rested in his lap. "Hi Brian, I'm David. Let's pick out some wheels for you."

Brian glanced at the images and shrugged. "What's the difference? A wheelchair is a wheelchair."

David laughed. "Oh, that's where you're wrong. I've learned a lot being in one for twenty years. A good wheelchair is like an extension of yourself."

Brian eyed him, a level of respect now filled him. "Twenty years? You've been in a wheelchair that long?" What he wanted to ask was how? Why?

As if he knew the unvoiced question in his mind, David answered him. "Motorcycle crash. I had a helmet on, but it snapped my spine. Haven't felt anything from my chest down since."

Motorcycles. Something else Brian hadn't thought about since becoming an amputee. "That sucks. I love bikes. Own four of them. I guess I'm going need to sell them when I get out of this place."

"It changed my life, that's for sure. But now you don't have to learn how to pick out wheelchairs through trial and error like I did."

David flipped through the catalog. He eyed Brian. "Everyone starts out wanting something that looks cool, but first we need to find ones that fit your lifestyle."

Looks cool? Yeah, right. Brian snorted. "I'm an airplane mechanic. Got something in there that will help me fix planes?"

The older man gave him an apologetic look and nodded. "I'd just signed a letter of intent to play football for Colorado. You'll adapt." He turned the page and pointed to a picture. "You're a young guy, and you're active. You'll want something lightweight, compact, easy to lift by yourself." He pointed to Brian's bandaged wrist stump. "This one you'd even be able to disassemble without help."

THIRTY-SEVEN

....

BACK ON YOUR FEET

Later that week, Brian wheeled himself into the therapy room in a shiny new metallic blue wheelchair. He transferred himself onto the therapy table and strapped weights onto his ankle. From his side, he performed a series of leg-lifts designed to strengthen his weakened muscles.

Renee approached with a pair of plastic splints attached to high-top leather shoes. "Now the work really starts."

She helped Brian strap the prosthetics onto his legs and fasten the Velcro on the shoes. Brian eyed the parallel walking assist bars across the room. He raised his right arm and looked at her. "How's this supposed to work? I can't hold on to a bar."

His nurse laughed. She raised a finger and an eyebrow. Renee left a moment and returned with a walker. A plastic platform for his right arm was attached to it. "Got it covered. Let's give it a try."

She helped Brian stand. Together, they took a few awkward steps. He winced as sharp fire-like pain stabbed at what was left of his feet. "Ouch. Is it supposed to hurt?"

Renee nodded, but didn't stop walking. "It's like learning to play a guitar. You have to get calluses on your stumps, and get used to the pain."

He took a few more unsteady steps with her help. "I'm taller in these things than I was in tennis shoes."

She made a non-committal sound. "It might take you a while to get used to balancing on the prosthetics. We'll walk twice a day. Every day."

Twice a day? He wanted to go home, and soon. He'd walk all day if it would help him get there any sooner. Pain or no pain.

Renee's words about giving his grafted stumps some time to develop calluses made sense when he started getting open pressure sores on the tender skin covering his remaining foot bones. But it didn't take him long to go from needing her help to stand to being able to make a lap around the lounge unassisted.

Between using the walker and his wheelchair, Brian got to know some of the other patients on the unit. Guys with head injuries who struggled with speech and coordination. Memory problems. The man in the halo traction who would never walk or move his arms again. It made losing his feet and hand seem almost petty in comparison.

It also helped to have some card playing buddies to pass the time. That's where he sat, the mid-afternoon sun streaming through the big picture window on the west wall of the lounge, when he noticed Dad coming toward him. *What the hell? In the middle of a week?* That didn't make any sense. Dad only came down on the weekends. Brian sat his cards down as he approached.

"Your mom's in the hospital. She's got to have surgery."

"What? Slow down, you know I can't hear very good." Surely he had to be missing something here.

"She stepped in a pothole and broke her ankle. Where's your walker? We need to go." Dad glanced around as if he'd brought both his wheelchair and walker out into the lounge.

Brian's initial fear and shock gave way to relief that it was only a broken bone. Mom was tough. She'd heal. When they arrived at the hospital, Brian was shocked to find his mom with her whole foot pointing at a right angle from the direction feet normally face.

Brian wheeled close to her bed and gave her a kiss. "I thought we usually did this the other way around. Me in the bed, and you holding my hand."

She barely chuckled, her eye distant and glazed. Brian assumed they'd given her some powerful pain medicine.

A doctor showed them a x-ray and explained Mom's injuries. A piece of the end of her tibia was broken and separated from the rest of the bone. She'd also dislocated the ankle, and would require surgery to screw everything back together.

Dad might have aged a decade with the stress, but eventually things got back to normal. Brian did have a new appreciation for what it must have been like for his family when it had been him on the other side of things.

* * *

Another step in getting home took place soon after. Brian sat in his wheelchair in the Hangar Prosthetics Consultation room as a technician slid a flesh-colored hard plastic prosthetic with a silver hook over the stump of his right wrist. It covered his arm all the way to the elbow and had an inner silicone plastic sleeve to cushion his skin. He twisted it a few times as he inspected it. Heavy, but manageable.

"Flex your muscles like you are opening your hand." The tech mimicked the motion he wanted Brian to use with his own hand. Brian nodded and tried to think about opening and closing his fingers. To his surprise, as his muscles moved, the hook opened and closed. "That's pretty cool!"

He turned the arm and practiced opening and closing the hook a few more times, then tried to pick up a pen from the table beside him. Okay, so he'd need to practice this a bit, but not bad. Not bad at all.

Now Renee wanted him to learn how to walk without the walker. It wasn't nearly as easy as Brian hoped it might be. He spent what seemed like endless hours traversing the few feet of parallel bars in the Physical Therapy room. Distance approximation and balance still dealt him fits. He'd miss his grip on the bar with the hook, or stumble and fall. Instead of rushing over to help him up, Renee stood off to the side and watched him get back to his feet. No matter how much he glared at her.

I've been walking since before I was a year old. It pissed him off. His anger made him work that much harder. Before long, he could get his leg splints and shoes on using his left hand and the hook. Wear regular jeans with button waists and zippers. And, walk without needing a walker.

The next phases of rehabilitation involved learning how to drive a car again. It took a while to figure out how to make the prosthetic feet behave on the pedals. Toes bend. The rigid brace and shoe? Not so much.

Brian's first driving trip alone reminded him of the exhilaration of his first solo airplane flight. He rolled down the car windows and let the wind blow. Nothing but him and the road.

Freedom. Once he had the ability to drive when and where he wanted, Brian didn't hesitate to use it. Not too long after, the rehab team decided he was ready to go home for real. *Probably tired of trying to chase me down for therapy sessions.*

THIRTY-EIGHT

....

HOME

Outside of Amy's house–even though he was going to be living there, he couldn't bring himself to call it *his* house–Brian transferred himself from the car into his wheelchair. Using his legs and feet, he propelled the wheelchair to the front door as Amy beamed at him. He stood up long enough to kiss her.

Inside, from the wheelchair, he looked around. Nothing had changed from the last time he'd been there. *Amy's house.* Jessie jumped up into his lap. He petted her soft fur while she licked his hand. "Where's all my stuff?"

Amy carried in one of his bags and set it on the floor. "Oh. Most of it is in the basement."

A jolt of anger flashed through Brian. "That's convenient." He tried to keep the sarcasm out of his voice, but failed.

Amy smiled. "It's crowded enough up here. I've got everything we need."

He shook his head and wheeled to the bathroom. There was no way his wheelchair was ever going to fit through the narrow door. There was a white plastic shower stool to sit on, but it was going to be a challenge in the middle of the night when he had to pee. He called over his shoulder, "My apartment closet was bigger than your whole bathroom."

He couldn't shake the sense of frustration that swallowed him whole. He'd thought being discharged would be a happy occasion. Instead, why did it seem as if he'd just received a jail sentence? A lifetime jail sentence at that. He wheeled himself to the window and stared outside as the wind whipped dry brown leaves through the quiet street.

* * *

Figuring out his finances was his first concern.

Brian wheeled himself into the drab Social Security office with a stack of papers clutched in his hook. A stern older woman with her gray hair pulled into a tight bun eyed him from behind the desk. She took the stack of papers from him, frowned when she saw that some of the pages were crumpled, and thumbed through them. "You'll get a notification of when your hearing will be held."

Say what? "Hearing?"

"It's standard procedure. You'll go before a judge and he'll decide if you're disabled."

Oh, you have to be kidding. Brian held up his right arm. "You mean the wheelchair, fake feet, hearing aide, and hook aren't enough?"

The woman placed the forms into a manila folder. She rapped the papers on her desk a couple of times without giving him a second glance. "The hearing will be in about six months."

"What the hell am I supposed to do with no income for six months?" He hated having to depend on Amy for everything. It already seemed like she looked down on him–treated him like a child. Six months without income? That wasn't going to work at all.

The woman gave him a sympathetic smile over the top of her wire reading glasses. "I'm sorry. Standard procedures."

* * *

Brian opened the front door to Amy's house and let in his friends. Kevin carried in a twelve-pack of beer and placed it on the coffee table. He and Hal took seats on the couch.

Kevin handed a beer to Brian before opening one for himself. He glanced around the living room. "Where's Amy?"

Brian took a deep swig of beer. He hadn't had one since before he'd gotten sick. Never was much of a drinker, but damn, it tasted good. He shrugged. "She's working. She's always either at the nursing home or in class."

Kevin grinned. "Shit, so you get the place to yourself? That's not all bad."

Brian snorted. "You'd think so, wouldn't you?"

Hal leaned forward and looked at him. "So, what are you going to do now, Brian?"

Leave it to the boss to get right to the point.

"I don't know." And Brian didn't have a clue, either. He took another long drink and let the carbonation burn the back of his throat. "But I need to do something other than just sit around here all day. I'm going out of my fucking mind."

Hal scratched his head. "You're still on a medical leave of absence from Duncan, aren't you?"

Brian held up his arm. "And how am I supposed to fix airplanes with a hook and a wheelchair?"

"But you still work for the company. Maybe they can find you a desk job?"

Maybe? He hadn't given it serious thought, but if Hal thought he could, maybe it was worth looking into. "I need to find something, so I can tell Social Security to fuck off."

* * *

The next morning, Brian sat in his wheelchair in front of Georgia, Duncan's Human Resources manager. The salt and pepper haired woman shuffled some papers on her desk and looked up at him. "I don't know what we have for openings right now, but if we don't find something for you by the six-month mark, you'll be out of LOA time."

Brian leaned forward. *Out of leave time?* "What happens then?"

Georgia gave him a kindly but sad smile. "We'd have to let you go."

Brian shook his head, fear flowing through him in cold waves. "Great. How long do I have?"

She typed on her computer keyboard and put her reading glasses on to view the screen. "Looks like we have until October sixth to either find you a job you can do, or terminate your employment. That's two weeks from today."

Brian sighed and slouched in his chair. He'd even dressed up today in his work uniform. It hadn't been an easy deal to get the damned thing buttoned, either.

Georgia surveyed his scarred hand and hook prosthesis. "Can you type?"

Next was an interview with James Prater. Another desk, with more paper shuffling. James gave Brian a penetrating stare. "I really don't know if we have any desk jobs you'd be qualified for right now."

Brian didn't want to have to beg for a job, but surely he had some skills that would continue to make him valuable to the company. Valuable enough to warrant a job. "I'm good at fixing planes, and I know the FAA regulations and paperwork."

His boss folded his arms and surveyed him. "Most of the guys on the floor will never do anything but fix planes."

Brian couldn't argue with that. Hell, six months ago, he planned on repairing aircraft for the rest of his life. Things change. "Most of them don't want to. I don't have any choice but to do something different, and I'd like it to be at Duncan. At least I'd still be working with planes." He stared at a framed photograph of a corporate jet on the wall for a moment before continuing. "Flying is my life. Always has been. Even if I'm behind a desk, at least I'm still part of it."

James took in a deep breath. He stared at the papers for a moment. "All right. We'll give it a try."

Brian tried to control himself. He had to resist the urge to jump up and yell.

"It's going to be temporary for now. You're young. Inexperienced." James raised a finger. "And don't think that wheelchair gets you a free pass."

All Brian needed was a medical release to return to work. He called and left a message with Dr. Hao's nurse. Then waited for the return call. Late in the afternoon, he lounged on the couch with his feet up. His splints sat on the floor beside him, along with his wheelchair, when his cell phone rang. Dr. Hao's number showed on the screen. "Hey, I need a release to go back to work."

The doctor's confused voice came through the receiver. "What will you be doing? Don't you fix planes?"

Brian grinned, in spite of himself. "I got an office job at Duncan."

Dr. Hao responded, "Your ITP has been very stable. But I see you have stopped going to physical therapy."

Brian snorted. "I know how far I can walk without my feet bleeding. I'm not wasting it going nowhere in PT."

"Always so stubborn."

The doctor had that much right. "Yup. How about a work release?"

Later, Brian sat on the edge of the bed. He pulled off his splints, socks, and the Band-Aid on his right foot. An open bloody area an inch in diameter covered the contact portion of his stump. He touched the tender surface. Who cared about a pressure sore? He had a job. And a job meant a paycheck. Insurance. The kind of things he'd need if he wanted to reclaim his life.

Something was missing. And Brian thought he knew where it was. He stared down the steep abyss leading to the basement. He'd managed to knock his wheelchair down there one day. Had to wait for Amy to get off work and haul it back up for him. He might not be able to get a wheelchair up a set of stairs, but this, he could manage. He lowered himself to the top stair and scooted down the steps on his butt. At the bottom, he walked the few feet across the partially-finished basement to a stack of boxes along the far wall.

Now, where is it? He shook his head in disgust as he dug through a couple of the boxes. *Who packed this stuff, anyway?* Did they even give a shit whether things broke or not? He caught sight of black vinyl and white plush. *Aha, found it!* Brian grabbed his Aviator Snoopy and carried it gently to the bottom of the stairs. Once there, he sat down, placed Snoopy an arm's reach above him, and raised himself up to the next rung. One step at a time, he moved his good luck charm up the staircase.

THIRTY-NINE

....

TROUBLE

Brian sat on the couch with his feet up and Jessie on his lap. Amy walked in the front door, her scrubs disheveled. She headed for the bedroom without even acknowledging them. Her irritated yell came from the bedroom. "God damn it. Did you forget to take her out again?"

Brian looked down at Jessie. The little dog wagged her tail. "I took her out twice. It's not exactly easy, you know."

Amy re-appeared in the doorway with a tissue in her hand. "I clean up pee and poop all day long. I don't want to come home and do it, too."

The distance between the two of them only grew. Brian had never been able to sleep if their bodies touched. He got too hot. Now, he struggled to sleep, even when she was as far away as possible on the other side of their king-sized bed. It might as well be the Sahara Desert separating them.

* * *

After yet another fight, Brian sat on the hood of his car in front of the Duncan hangars. He couldn't even remember what started this one. The approaching dusk brought out lights in green, red, white, and blue along the taxiways. He took the last sips of iced tea from a McDonald's cup, then pulled the straw out and fidgeted with it. On the runway across from him, a jet took off and climbed into the sky. Brian watched it until it disappeared into the distance. He crumpled the straw and threw it in his open car window. His cell phone vibrated in his pocket. Brian grinned when he saw Troy's number on the screen.

"Hey, Thomas, a bunch of us are heading to Yankton tonight. You should come."

All the way to Yankton? Tonight? Brian opened his mouth to say no, but then it hit him. He missed his friends.

A lot.

Maybe that was exactly what he needed. Some beers with friends and a few hours to take his mind off the growing problems with Amy. "Got some place I can crash tonight? It'll be late."

"Got you covered. Motel right next door to the bar."

Brian crawled into the driver's seat and positioned his thumb to hit Amy's number. His hand hovered in mid-air. Last thing he wanted was another fight. His fingers flew as he typed on the touch-screen. "Heading to Yankton to see the guys. Be back tomorrow. No charger, and my phone is dying."

As soon as he hit send, Brian switched the phone off. She'd be pissed. But, he'd deal with it tomorrow.

The miles of road between Lincoln and Yankton usually drove him nuts with boredom. Tonight, it was more as if he dropped an invisible weight in each town he passed through. The prospect of being with friends and laughing like they had in high school. Back then, life was so much easier, even with the ITP and all. The memories propelled him forward.

Being surrounded by Troy, Luke, Tim, and Jacob, Brian even managed to forget about his amputations for a while. Tim nudged him. "Things not so hot at home?"

Brian glanced at Troy, who waved his hands in an animated conversation with Luke and Jacob. *Troy never could keep his mouth shut.* "It happens. She's done so much for me, but..." Brian's voice trailed off.

Tim threw an arm over his shoulder. "Maybe it wasn't meant to be. Might be time to move on." He gestured with the long neck beer bottle in his hand to a table filled with women about their age.

Brian snorted and raised his hook. "Yeah, that's just what I need. Pity from beautiful women." He started to turn away when one of the girls turned her head. *Oh, shit.* He blinked and looked again. There was no doubt.

He recognized the brunette.

Kari.

Tim's eyes followed his gaze. "Isn't that–"

"Yes."

"Didn't you two–"

Brian cut him off again, "And it didn't end well." He spun in his chair and stared at the table. Maybe if he kept his back turned to her, she wouldn't notice him. Better yet, he should call it a night. From the number of beer bottles and pitchers on the table, it was a good thing he already had a room booked.

Even with his hearing muddled from the noise in the crowded bar, Brian sensed Kari's approach before her fingers traced his neck and covered his eyes. Her voice pierced the jumble of sound. "Guess who?"

Without thinking, Brian reached up to touch her hands. She flinched as his hook grazed her skin. He hadn't seen Kari since their break-up, while they were still in college. She probably had no idea he was an amputee.

"Jennifer Aniston?" He smiled in spite of himself. It had been a running joke of theirs that the *Friends* star was his 'celebrity free pass.'

The scent of her perfume wafted over him as she bent to kiss his cheek. He turned toward Kari. Her smile... her eyes... She hadn't changed a bit. Visions of late nights with the two of them tangled in the sheets of her bed flashed through his mind. Brian downed the last of his beer in attempt to drown the memory.

"Looks like this boy's ready for another." Jacob waved the waitress over. "And one for the lady, " he added, in spite of Brian's pointed glance. Jacob pulled a vacant chair from a nearby table and slid it next to Brian's.

As the night progressed, they laughed and talked, and her hand kept finding its way to his thigh. It was as if the breakup and intervening years between them disappeared. As the bartender announced last call, Brian stood. The neon lights swam around him.

Troy and Tim switched to ordering pitchers a while back, and to be honest, Brian had no idea how many times they'd filled his glass. Apparently, a few too many. He eyed his wheelchair, sitting against the wall. Why hadn't he parked it closer?

Kari squeezed his shoulder and jumped up. Before Brian had time to think, she wove through the bar patrons and collected his wheelchair. "You always had a thing for blue." She ran a finger along the painted frame.

Brian laughed. "Just blue eyes." His gaze locked on hers. He'd forgotten how they melded everything perfect about the sea and sky together. Her hand brushed against his back as he sat.

"You need me to come tuck you in, Thomas?" Jacob glanced over his shoulder toward Brian.

Brian shook his head. The room swam a bit, but he figured he could make it into a handicapped accessible room without too much trouble. Kari leaned in next to his good ear. "You staying next door? I'm parked right there, I'll walk with you."

Tim gave him a knowing glance. One Brian tried to ignore as he and Kari said their goodbyes and stepped into the cool South Dakota night. The short distance from the bar to the motel passed in quick silence. Once they reached the door, he glanced around. "Where's your car?"

Kari pointed to a Honda Civic a short distance away. She scuffed the toe of her high-heeled boot against the pavement a moment, then bent down and kissed him.

Without thinking, Brian wound his fingers through her hair and kissed her back.

FORTY

....

THE AFTERMATH

Brian cradled his coffee cup and stared at it. His gut clenched. *What have I done?*

As if giving voice to his fears, Kari dropped the straw she'd been chewing onto the table. "Now what?"

That was the million dollar question, wasn't it? Unfortunately, he didn't have a clue. "I'm living with Amy." The words came out harsh. Things were a mess with Amy, and this only made matters worse.

Kari avoided his eyes and fidgeted with her mangled straw. "So, that's it?"

Every horrible emotion Brian remembered from their breakup threatened to drown him. "I have to tell her."

Kari shook her head and blew out a deep breath. "Is she going to turn psycho?"

Another question he couldn't answer. Things had been building with Amy for a long time, but this wasn't how he wanted to end it.

Brian's brow furrowed. "You're not helping."

Every weight he'd shed on the trip north multiplied in his absence, and by the time Brian reached Lincoln, it threatened to crush him. In sight of Amy's house, he had to fight the urge to keep driving.

Brian wheeled himself inside where Amy sat curled up on the couch with the television on. She glared at him. "Thanks for letting me worry."

He moved his wheelchair closer to her. He took off his leg splints and clenched his teeth as he pulled off his socks. They'd stuck to the open areas on his feet again. But this wasn't about his feet. He took a deep breath and began, "I'm not the same guy I was before..." He held up his hook and blood-stained socks. "...all of this."

Amy gave him a wary frown. "And?"

He couldn't go back now. The words rushed out of his mouth so he wouldn't be tempted to change his mind. "I slept with someone last night."

Her mouth dropped open as the color drained from her face.

She dissolved into tears. He planned on anger. Temper, he could handle. *Why did she have to cry?*

"How could you do this? I stood by you through everything. I promised your folks I wouldn't leave you, and I haven't."

Brian tried to move closer to her, but Amy cowered behind a raised hand as if to fend him off. "Because you made a promise to my parents? Is that the only reason?" He had to admit to himself that part of him assumed a woman would never be attracted to him again. Was that why he let things get out of hand with Kari? Because she found him desirable in spite of the amputations?

Amy only cried harder.

"I'm sorry. I just happened–"

Amy's eyes flashed with fury. She cut off his attempted apology with a snort.

Brian tried again. "I'm not trying to excuse anything. I've been miserable since it happened."

"Stop talking. I don't want to hear it." Amy curled into a ball as racking sobs engulfed her. "I hate you... I hate you..." She repeated the words as she rocked herself.

Jessie jumped into his lap, oblivious to the tension. When he'd left for Yankton, his thoughts were that he and Amy just weren't meant to be together. They were like two strangers under the same roof most of the time. But now, he wanted more than anything to make things better with her. He tried to reach out for her, but she pulled away.

Tears flooded Brian's cheeks. He locked the wheelchair and crawled on his knees to the couch. "Can you forgive me? I'm so sorry. I'll do anything to make things right."

"I want you out." Amy stood up and glared at him. "And I don't want your fucking dog, either." She stomped to the bedroom and slammed the door.

Brian crumpled into a pile as his tears turned into quaking sobs.

FORTY-ONE

....

ON MY OWN

Kevin and Hal helped him move into an apartment he found after spending a couple of weeks in Hal's spare bedroom. Brian wheeled up to Hal's old Ford 250 pickup with a box in his lap. He handed it up to Hal in the pickup bed while Amy watched from the doorway. She held Jessie and cried, her eyes red and puffy.

Kevin came out with another box in his arms. "I think that's it." He looked back at Amy. "You going to go say something to her?"

What the hell was he supposed to say, anyway? Brian wheeled himself to the door. Unsure, he reached for Jessie. Amy handed the dog to him.

He stroked her soft fur and cuddled her close to his chest. Brian murmured into Jessie's ear, "I'll come visit, Jessie." He looked up at Amy. "Thanks for keeping her. It means a lot to me."

Amy scooped Jessie up and glared at him, her eyes full of ice. "I'm doing it for her. You couldn't take care of her anyway." She swatted the tears away from her cheeks. "You always loved this damned dog more than you did me."

Her words struck him like a slap. *One I deserve.*

* * *

Moving on meant moving on, and unfortunately, a few things needed to go. Brian sat in his wheelchair near the parking lot curb of his small brick apartment building. The roar of a motorcycle engine and flash of blue whizzed by, then swung into the parking lot next to him. Jeff, the guy test-driving his Yamaha FZR 400, lowered the kickstand and took off his helmet.

Brian eyed him. "Well, what do you think?"

Jeff nodded appreciatively. "You're right. She flies. These babies are rare. How'd you find it?"

A smile cracked Brian's face. "My brother was stationed in Okinawa. He shipped it to me in pieces. We put it back together when he was home on leave."

Jeff ran his hand along the handlebar. "It's a shame you have to get rid of it."Brian shrugged and lifted his hook. "What am I supposed to do with it?"

Once he'd sold the bikes and unpacked his few possessions, he made good on his promise to visit Jessie.

Amy hadn't seemed all that excited for him to stop over when he first mentioned it. Brian didn't really care. He was coming to see his dog, not her. He sat on the couch, still in his Duncan work uniform and his wheelchair nearby, while Jessie jumped up and licked him.

Dogs really did give unconditional love. It didn't matter that he'd been forced to leave her when he moved out, Jessie still loved him like nothing had ever happened. "Hey, Jessie. Did you miss me?"

Amy's voice called to him from the bedroom. "You should have called first."

"We talked about it last week."

Amy walked into the living room, her hair in hot rollers, wearing a dress. "I have a date, and I don't want you here when he comes to pick me up."

Fair enough. He continued to pet Jessie and ignored her. "Where's your toy, Jessie? Go get it."

Amy threw her hands up, her voice shrill, "That's it? Don't you even care?"

Yes, he cared, and yes, he deserved her anger. But he couldn't keep his own pain from clouding his words. Brian looked up at her. "You didn't waste any time, but no. Not really. Am I supposed to?"

She stomped into the bathroom and slammed the door behind her.

FORTY-TWO

··

FREE-FALL

Brian wheeled himself into his apartment living room. He didn't have a lot for furniture, which was a blessing. Less to get in the way of his wheelchair. A blue couch on one wall and a big screen television on the other filled most of the space. Posters of scenery he'd photographed from airplanes hung on the walls.

He transferred himself to the couch and took off his leg splints. He threw his legs up, using his wheelchair as an ottoman, picked up his laptop, and logged into Facebook. An ad at the margin caught his eye. Brian clicked on the link. A smile spread across his face as he looked at the screen. *Now this could be fun.*

That weekend, Brian pulled his car up to a hangar at the Crete Airport. An old beat-up Cessna 182 sat nearby. He climbed out of the car, grabbed his wheelchair from the trunk, and wheeled himself to the door.

Inside, he shook hands with Blake, the tall muscular jump master. "You must be Brian Thomas. I'm Blake. We talked on the phone." The jump master eyed the wheelchair and Brian's prosthetic arm. "You said you can walk and get around in the plane, but I'm not sure about the hook."

Brian held it up and looked at it. "Yeah, I'd hate to drop a forty thousand dollar prosthetic from ten thousand feet."

Blake laughed. "I was more worried about getting hit in the head with it."

Brian rapped on it with his left hand. "Good point. It might hurt a little. We'd better leave it on the ground."

Blake motioned to the office area of the hangar. "I have just a few forms to fill out before we get started."

Brian followed him and parked his wheelchair next to an old metal desk. Lockers lined one wall, and parachutes hung from the ceiling. What looked like an old wrestling mat covered a section of the concrete floor. Blake pulled out a stack of papers and plopped them in front of him. "This is where you basically promise not to sue us if you plummet to your death or get injured." He thumbed through the pile. "In only about fifty short signatures."

Brian laughed. "Compared to what I've been through the past year, jumping out of an airplane is safe."

Brian signed his initials and name more times than he possibly had since learning how to write with his left hand. Then he walked up and down the length of the hangar for Blake to assess his gait. *Not a problem.* He changed into a jumpsuit and learned how to hold his body during the jump itself. It involved getting down onto the mat and laying on his stomach with his arms and feet lifted. Brian hadn't realized how much strength and flexibility it would take to hold the position on the ground. Blake assured him it would be a lot easier during freefall, since the wind would help keep his extremities in the correct position.

After the training, Blake changed into his own jumpsuit, and they were off to the plane. Brian wheeled himself out to the waiting Cessna and climbed inside. All of the seats except the pilot's had been removed to make more room for the sky divers and their gear. Blake climbed in behind him.

As the pilot prepared for takeoff, Blake leaned toward him. "Why do you want to jump out of a perfectly good airplane, anyway?"

Brian shook his head and grinned. "I'm an airplane mechanic. Trust me, there's no such thing as a perfectly good airplane."

Blake laughed and nodded.

Brian continued. "I got my pilot's license when I was still in high school, but I can't fly legally now. I've flown plenty of planes, but never jumped out of one before. Figured, fuck it, why not?"

The airplane rumbled to life. Brian grinned as it taxied out for takeoff. Blake looked at an altimeter on his wrist and leaned towards Brian's ear. "We'll jump from ten thousand five hundred feet. Its gonna be cold with the door open." He grinned. "But it won't be cold for long."

Once airborne and at the proper altitude, Brian kneeled beside the door as Blake connected their jump harnesses. The door flew open. Brian stared out at the wide open expanse below them. Their breath was visible until it trailed outside the plane, then it abruptly cut off, pulled away with the fast rush of air as the plane soared through the sky.

This was it.

Brian's heart raced, adrenaline-fueled excitement flooded his senses. Joined by the harness, the pair leaned out the door and less jumped than basically fell into the sky.

The freefall was like nothing he'd ever experienced. Quite possibly every pilot dreamed of soaring like an eagle. Really flying, instead of simply steering something like a car on wings. This must be what birds experienced. The resistance of the air gave him a sense of buoyancy, almost as if he were floating.

All too soon, Blake pulled the parachute cord, and a rapid tug jerked them upward. The chute deployed above them in a multicolored expanse over their heads.

Only now, suspended in mid-air and floating at the end of a harness, could Brian really absorb the sights around him. The neat patterns of the plowed fields, cut into squares by bisecting roads, the gentle rippling waves through the crops as the wind rustled through them. *Was the sky always this blue?* Even though Blake was tethered right behind him, his breath warm against Brian's neck, he still had the sensation of it being nothing but him, alone with the world.

Blake's tap on his shoulder pulled him from his thoughts. Brian looked down at the rapidly approaching ground and pulled his legs up in a sitting position, like he'd practiced in the hangar. Together, he and Blake made a sliding landing.

Blake helped Brian from the ground as the pilot brought the wheelchair up to them. Brian pumped his fist into the air. "That was awesome!"

Blake slapped him on the back. "Told you so, Buddy. More fun than flying?

The pilot handed Brian his arm prosthesis. He slipped it on his bare stump."Doesn't last long enough. I could fly all day." He grinned. "Still, not bad."

FORTY-THREE

....

A HOOK AND A PRAYER

Something changed for Brian after the skydiving trip. He'd spent all of his time since his illness trying to hide his disabilities. He hated it when people stared at him. Some guy even tried to pay for his dinner one night, thinking he was a disabled veteran. Every time you met someone new, there was the same round of questions. *How'd it happen? What does it feel like? How does the hook work? Does everything else work okay? Do you have a job?* It made meeting anyone to date more than challenging. Most of the time, he preferred to simply grab something take-out, and stay at home.

But, if he could jump out of an airplane, why couldn't he go out and have fun? *Why not? It's all in the attitude, right?* Kevin had been asking him to come hang out some Friday night ever since he came back to work, so this time, instead of making an excuse, he agreed to meet him at the bar. Now it had become almost an unspoken expectation of their weekend routine.

Brian had already been at the bar for a while when Kevin got there. The mechanic had texted and said he would be late. He had a plane that had been promised to go out, and the client needed a few last minute tweaks to the plane. Brian remembered very well those last-minute pushes, being a mechanic on the floor. Now, as a tech writer, he was responsible for making sure paperwork was ready to go when the client came to pick up the plane. And the first one in the line of fire if it wasn't. It didn't matter. He took the time to grab a burger and a beer while he waited.

He sat at the end of the bar counter in the busy nightclub. Bright brass and hardwood illuminated by soft lights graced the bar top. He'd even had time to get to know his waitress a bit. Melanie. She was a tiny thing in her tight jeans and a low cut tank top, and she made it a point to walk by him with a swish of her long brunette ponytail as often as she could. Certainly more than she needed to. As Kevin headed to his table, she passed by Brian and brushed her hand across his shoulder. He grinned and nodded as Kevin joined him.

His friend whistled under his teeth. "Sympathy must work wonders."

Brian laughed. "The hook gets their attention, the smile gets them talking, but the story gets their clothes off."

Kevin snorted. "You wish, Buddy."

Brian raised an eyebrow. "Watch this."

As she passed by, Brian nodded and smiled to get her attention. "Hey, Melanie, how about a refill for me, and fix this sorry asshole up with a round?" He twisted the hook off the base of his prosthesis and clamped it to the handle of his empty beer mug. "Here, now you'll know which glass is mine."

The pretty waitress shook her head and laughed as she took his mug to the tap. While she filled his beer, it came loose from the mug handle. She pulled it off and looped it through the scoop in her tank top and bra. When Melanie returned with the beer mugs on a tray, the hook hung in her cleavage.

Brian grinned as he eyed her. "You could leave it there all night. I wouldn't complain."

She pulled it from her top and handed it to him. "I think your hook has felt me up enough for one night, Mister."

Brian feigned pain as he took the titanium hook from her and reattached it to the rest of the prosthesis on his arm. "Oh, that hurts. Painful."

Melanie laughed and shook her head as she walked away to wait on another table. Kevin fanned himself. "Wow. That's almost enough to make me wish I had a claw like you." He raised a finger. "Note, I said 'almost'."

FORTY-FOUR

....

SEATTLE

One nice thing about being back at work besides getting a steady paycheck–and a nice raise after he'd finished his probationary period–was collecting vacation time. When Dana suggested he come out to Washington State, Brian didn't think twice before he accepted. Not even the thought of driving half-way across the country alone bothered him. Open spaces always made him happy. Plus, if he planned it well, he could stop off in Denver and see Corey on the way, too.

So, here he was, driving through eastern Colorado as dusk played off the distant hint of foothills. He'd forgotten how close you had to get to Denver before you actually realized you were in the Rocky Mountains. Right now, it looked exactly like western Nebraska. In other words, a whole lot of flat.

The goal was to make it to Corey's before it got too much later. The thought of navigating through Denver after dark already wasn't all that appealing, even with a GPS. A wrong turn could easily land you in a neighborhood you really didn't want to be in. He had to laugh a little bit as he imagined a headline saying, *Triple Amputee Shot Dead in Gang War, Didn't Hear Warnings.*

Brian kicked off both of his leg braces somewhere around Sidney, Nebraska. With cruise control, it wasn't like he really needed them on, and he might as well give his feet a rest. He left them in the seat next to him so they'd be easy to grab and put on when he needed a pit stop.

Flashing lights appeared behind him. Brian glanced at the speedometer and drew in a sharp breath. "Shit."

Well, when you were caught, you were caught. Nothing to do but pull over. The Colorado State Trooper got out of his police cruiser and approached Brian's driver's window. "In a hurry?"

Brian handed the trooper his license and registration. "Sorry, I wasn't paying attention to how fast I was going."

A white cone of light flicked through the car, and over his leg braces, hook, and the wheelchair in his back seat. He scrutinized Brian's license, then looked at him. "How long you been in the wheelchair?"

"A few months."

The man shook his head. "I wondered. You still have a motorcycle endorsement on here." He pulled out his ticket book and scribbled on a form, tore it from the pad and handed it to Brian, along with his license and registration.

Brian held his breath as he looked at it. How much was this going to cut out of his vacation budget? Did Colorado make you pay your ticket on the spot? Worse yet, would he have to drive back out for a court date?

There wasn't a fine listed on the form.

A warning? Really? Brian's head jerked up in surprise. "Thanks!"

The trooper's military-like composure broke for a brief moment. He even cracked what might have been the smallest of a smile. Or, it could have just been an illusion created by the shadows from the spotlight on the cruiser. "Slow down, Son."

"No ticket?"

The trooper pushed his Mounties-style felt hat back on his head and looked in at him, a look of half-amused shock on his face. "What? You want one?"

"Hell no. Never gotten a warning before." The words rushed out before Brian had a chance to even think about how they sounded.

Luckily, the trooper just laughed and walked back to his cruiser.

* * *

The rest of the trip turned out rather uneventful, as far as having any more misadventures with law enforcement. But then again, the fancy radar detector he bought before he left Denver might have helped, too. Now past the Rocky Mountains, and on the Seattle Interstate, the majestic snow-covered peak of Mount Rainier dominated the landscape. Brian detoured a bit to get a better view of the Space Needle. He'd have to convince Dana to come down and see it up close with him before his vacation ended.

The GPS guided him to Dana's house. Brian pulled his wheelchair out of the back seat as his brother came outside, along with his wife, Edith, and their two sons.

Dana gave him a quick hug, then took Brian's bags from the trunk. He handed one to each of his sons, even though the bags were nearly as large as the kids. The pair giggled and jostled each other as they lugged them inside behind their mother. Dana turned to him and grinned. "You tired after all that driving?"

Brian stretched and resisted the urge to yawn. Not that he was really all that tired, but why was it when someone mentioned being tired, you suddenly had the urge to yawn? "Not too bad, why?"

Dana looked up at the clear afternoon sky. "I looked at the weather. Thought you might want to check out Seattle from the air."Brian smiled and stood tall. He wasn't tired. Not when it meant being in a plane, and getting to see the mountains, Puget Sound, and the Pacific Ocean from the air.

Last time he'd come to visit them, he'd flown commercial. It wasn't the same at all. Yeah, jumbo airliners made the trip a whole lot faster, but they had to fly so high, you couldn't really see much. Even if you could make anything out from those fishbowl-like miniature windows. Not like a small aircraft, where you almost had a perfect 360 panoramic view. Close enough to make out all of the details of the landscape.

Brian grabbed his camera and grinned. "Let's do it!"

It didn't take them long to get to the airport and complete the pre-flight check of Dana's Cessna 172. His brother even let him take the pilot's left-side seat. From the right-sided co-pilot's seat, Dana opened the throttle and took off.

Brian busied himself taking photographs through the plane window–of the city below and Mount Rainier in the distance. Dana maneuvered the plane to help him get the best angles. "Think you've got enough pictures?"

Brian put his camera in his lap and looked at him, a little disappointed. "I suppose. We going back already?"

His brother shook his head, a mischievous smile on his face. "Think you can fly her, Little Brother?"

Brian didn't waste another moment. He reached out and grabbed the yoke as Dana released the one on the co-pilot's side. He banked the plane hard to the left. "Whoohoo! Hang on, Old Man."

Of course, the Cessna wasn't like flying with the Thunderbirds or the Blue Angels, but damn, that's what was on Brian's mind. He put the little bird through its paces while Dana sat back and watched him.

They stayed out probably longer than Dana had planned, but luckily, Edith didn't seem too upset at waiting dinner for them. "I wondered how you'd do with the rudder and brake pedals, but you handled it fine." Dana passed him a dish.

Brian scooped a healthy portion onto his plate. "Yeah, but my hearing is a problem. I couldn't hear what air traffic control was saying. They talk so fast."

Dana shrugged. "Get a better headset."

Brian had forgotten the real problem. "And the medical certification? I don't have one, you know. "

"Your platelets have been normal ever since you got sick."

That much was true. Brian still held his breath every time he noticed a bruise of any sort, and certainly every time he had blood drawn. "Yup, almost three years now. Hematologist thinks I might be cured."

"I'd look into if I was you. Pilots got to fly."

Brian jerked as Edith slapped a wooden spoon on the table. The boys, who had been steadily getting louder at the end of the table jumped in their seats. With mock sternness, Dana pointed toward his sons. The pair poked each other and giggled. "Table manners, you two."

FORTY-FIVE

···

WHY NOT?

Brian thought about Dana's words all the way home from Seattle. *Pilots got to fly.* But was it nuts to think it might be a possibility? There was no way he could fly solo without a current medical certificate, but it wouldn't hurt to look into it. Maybe brush up on some of the skills he hadn't used in a while with a flight instructor.

He asked around and looked online for flight instructors. One thing he listened for in the comments he got was for someone who liked a challenge. It was going to take someone willing to think outside the box a bit to take on a triple amputee with hearing loss, and Brian knew it. A few phone calls later, and he had a time to fly set up.

Now Brian stood beside a Cessna 152 as the flight instructor, a young guy named Mark, walked over to him.

Mark thrust out his hand. "You must be Brian Thomas."

Brian shook Mark's hand, pleased to see that the instructor didn't so much as bat an eye when he extended his left hand. "That's me."

Mark crossed his arms and looked Brian up and down, along with his wheelchair. He shook his head. "This ought to be interesting. Can't say as I've ever flown with anyone quite like you."

Brian nodded. "My brother says I did pretty good with his plane, even with all my modifications." He surveyed the Cessna. "I've never flown a 152. Looks nicer than what I'm used to."

Once they were airborne, Brian wasn't sure how to take the guy. Mark looked like he might be taking a nap half the time. Didn't say much, unless Brian specifically asked him a question.

Brian flew around a bit, trying to anticipate what the instructor might want him to demonstrate. Not that Mark seemed to be too concerned one way or the other.

After a few awkward minutes, Brian quit thinking about the flight instructor in the copilot seat. *Fuck it. I'm flying a plane. Paying to fly a plane. Just have fun!* Before long, it was like he was back in Springfield. He could almost imagine the football team out on the field, and him buzzing Homecoming games and graduations. Nothing but him and the sky, and the roar of a plane.

The time passed much too quickly. Brian landed the airplane smoothly and taxied to the hangar. He and Mark pulled off their headsets and crawled out of the plane. The flight instructor scribbled on a piece of paper and handed it to Brian. "Your radio communication needs work, but this guy specializes in special needs medical certification cases. Give him a call. Tell him I sent you."

* * *

Brian prepared before talking to the Aviation Medical Examiner, and for about two weeks he collected all of his medical records for the last five years. A boring process which involved faxing of release forms to previous medical facilities with copies of his driver's license and waiting for the documents to arrive in the mail. Then he scanned the nearly 900 pages worth of documents to digital format.

He emailed a doctor from Illinois on a Sunday evening asking for guidance, and within fifteen minutes had a reply. Brian read the email half shocked. The doctor listed instructions on how he wanted Brian to share his medical files online, and said he would start looking at them right away.

A week had passed when Brian got a phone call from the doctor. "I don't see anything disqualifying in your records, but we need a letter from your hematologist about ITP status, and some supporting lab work before I submit the report."

Hope?

"Then what?" Brian tried to hold back his excitement as he answered.

"Assuming the FAA grants your authorization, you take a medical flight evaluation at the Flight Standards District Office of your choice."

A moment of fear flashed through Brian. It had been a while. Would his flying skills be up to par for the FAA Inspector who administered the exam?

Weeks passed without word.

Every day, Brian checked the mailbox to find the typical junk and bills. Today, he spotted a thin envelope with an FAA return address. Brian held the envelope in his shaking hand. He'd been through this before—and not in a good way, either. *The FAA giveth, and the FAA taketh away.* Which would it be today?

He blew out a deep breath. Good God. He'd jumped out of an airplane. He could damn well take whatever was inside the letter. Brian yanked the envelope open and pulled out the sheet of paper inside. "Dear Mr. Thomas, We are pleased to inform you that you have been granted authorization to take medical flight evaluation..."

Now his hand shook.

All he needed was to pass the check flight with an FAA inspector. *Piece of cake.*

He hoped.

FORTY-SIX

··

CHECK FLIGHT

Inspector O'Connell stood beside the small airplane as he waited for his next check flight. The last one had been an utter disaster. Little bitty slip of a woman, he hadn't been sure whether she was more afraid of him or the plane. Heaven help her if she ever really hit turbulence. The few little bumps she had run into made her shake so hard he finally had to step in and help her. She'd been more than happy to hand the controls over to him, too. Not the thing you could afford to do when lives might depend on you. He'd sent her back for more flight instruction, even when she cried.

O'Connell's cell phone rang. He pulled it from the leather holster on his belt and answered it. "O'Connell here."

Not surprisingly, it was the office. He pulled a small calendar and pen from his jacket pocket. "Check flight for a triple amputee with profound hearing loss? You're wasting my time." He stuck his fingers in his ears as a Cessna roared overhead.

***

Brian pulled the yoke as the Cessna took off. He glanced over at Mark, who sat in the co-pilot's seat. "Do it again?"

Mark nodded. "Yup. This time do a simulated engine failure ."

Brian nodded. He banked the plane into the pattern. Below him, a man in a white shirt and flight jacket stood beside another plane talking on his cell phone.

* * *

You've flown tons of hours. You can do this in your sleep.

Just. Fly. The. Damned. Plane.

Funny how the knot in his stomach refused to listen to all of this logic.

Still in his work uniform, Brian stood outside the security door and waited to be buzzed into the Flight Standards District Office. He hoped leaving his wheelchair in the car was the right decision. Finally, a thin older guy with a white shirt and leather bomber jacket approached and let him in.

The man adjusted the wire glasses on his nose and looked at him, then his clip board. "Medical flight evaluation? Thomas?"

Brian extended his left hand to the man. "That would be me. Brian Thomas."

O'Connell flinched as he shook Brian's scarred hand.

"I'm Inspector O'Connell. The maintenance inspectors need to review the maintenance records and look over the airplane before we can fly."

The two walked back to an empty room. O'Connell took the airplane records from Brian and disappeared.

Brian didn't have time to study the records of the plane he'd rented to take his test flight. His stomach tied in knots as four other inspectors sat quietly in an adjacent room scouring them.

Finally, O'Connell returned. "Records look good. I'll meet you at the airplane."

Brian rolled around the airplane and waited in the cold November morning air. O'Connell and the other four inspectors pulled up in a car. The men took no time getting down to business. Each of them took turns examining the airplane. They crawled inside and out looking for reasons to stop the flight.

After they finished, O'Connell nodded. "Everything looks okay. I'll just watch you do your pre-flight." A smile crept across Brian's face. "I use some non-standard methods during my pre-flight. You don't report OSHA violations, do you?"

The inspector's head jerked up. "I need to know you can safely pre-flight before we even consider getting off the ground."

I'll take that as a no. Brian wheeled close to the wing of the plane, where the gas tanks were located. He locked his wheelchair and climbed up to stand on the seat like a ladder and checked the fuel levels.

Brian glanced over his shoulder to see O'Connell nod reluctantly. He grinned, circled the plane, and completed the remainder of the pre-flight inspection.

"Not bad. A bit unconventional, but you covered everything." O'Connell jotted a note on his logbook.

Once they'd strapped themselves into their seats, Brian fumbled with his headset as O'Connell scrutinized him. He'd followed Dana's advice and gotten a better one. And today, it didn't seem to be working correctly.

Brian scowled as he checked the connections to the intercom system. "Check, check." He unplugged the jack, reinserted it, and adjusted the microphone again.

O'Connell tapped his arm, his face concerned. "Is everything okay over here?"

Brian pointed to his ear. "I've got my hearing aide out. Can't hear you until I get the intercom going." He frowned. Everything was hooked up correctly, and the system worked fine on every other flight he'd taken. *What the hell?*

His mind ran through a troubleshooting scenario. *Aha.* Brian picked up the headset's noise cancelling unit and grabbed his flight bag. Batteries might be dead. It was always the simple things, right? He changed the AA batteries in the unit and re-placed the cover. "Check, check." He nodded. Live with sound. "That's better."

O'Connell nodded.

Brian turned the key and started the engine. It chugged a few moments, then sputtered and died. He gave O'Connell a sheepish look. "It's a little touchy sometimes." He adjusted the throttle knob and restarted the engine. It sputtered a while and died again.

Brian took a deep breath. "Third time's a charm right?" He pumped the throttle while the engine cranked and finally, the air-plane then roared to life.

O'Connell made another note in the log book.

Brian's heart raced in his chest, adrenaline threatening to ex-plode like nitroglycerine in his veins.

Once airborne, he flew the plane while O'Connell scrutinized him. The inspector's gaze lingered on Brian's hook, feet, and body position.

Brian had to ask O'Connell to repeat his instructions almost every time he talked. The guy had one of those voices he had difficulty hearing. And every time, it seemed to Brian a little more frustration crept into the inspector's voice.

Brian reached for the throttle knob with his hook. He tried to close his grip on it, but nothing happened.

A flash of fear crossed the inspector's face as his eyes widened. "Did that thing malfunction?" O'Connell jabbed a bony finger in the direction of Brian's hook.

Brian tried to flex his arm muscles a couple of times without a response from the prosthesis. "I think the battery died."

O'Connell reached for the throttle. "That's a problem. I'll get us back on the ground, and we'll call it a day."

Before he could reach the knob, Brian adjusted the clutch on the side of the prosthesis with his left hand. He cleanly pulled the throttle to the desired setting with the hook in the partially-closed position. "That's okay, I've got it. I ran entire flights with my instructor simulating a dead hook."

The inspector looked surprised and scribbled in his log. "How's your control using your feet?"

Brian shrugged. "How about I show you?"

He tried not to smile as he executed a series of tight banks, turns, and changes in elevation. For good measure, he even threw in a few practice emergencies as O'Connell watched him. He'd planned for all of the things he might be asked to do, and a bunch more. Maneuvers he'd need to be able to do when he was alone in the plane.

Then it was time to land and end the flight. Brian always loved the sensation of the plane descending for landing, and this was no exception. The wheels touched down as smooth as if they'd skidded onto polished glass. It didn't get any cleaner than that, and he knew it.

Brian taxied the plane back to the front of the hangar. He and Inspector O'Connell climbed out of the plane and stood beside it.

O'Connell cleared his throat and looked him in the eye. "I have to tell you, I'm surprised. I didn't think you'd be able to do it. But Son, you can fly."

"I had an old Cessna 150 a lot like this one when I was in high school. I traded it for a motorcycle when I moved to Lincoln." Brian lifted his hook. "Then I ended up like this. Motorcycles don't work well for amputees. But a plane? I can handle it fine."

O'Connell's staid expression softened a bit. "You know, this airplane used to be mine. Couldn't believe it when I saw the call letters today. I sold it few months ago. I'm glad I got to fly in it again." He patted the wing of the plane. Then he glanced at Brian, and a hint of a smile played at his mouth. "Welcome back, Pilot. Let's get the paperwork finished."

Later that evening, Brian caught himself opening his flight log just to look at the certificate. It was really there. He could fly again.

Why was he even bothering to try to watch television, anyway? Brian pulled out his iPad and checked the weather reports. A beautiful November evening, low wind, clear sky. *Why not?* A couple of phone calls later, and he was back out the door with his flight bag on his lap.

The automatic doors at Duncan Aviation swished open as his wheelchair approached. Brian stopped in front of the reception desk overlooking the airfield. The night desk clerk, Megan, looked up at him. She smiled as he filled out the log book on the counter. "Are you flying with someone tonight?"

There would be plenty of time to take up passengers. "Not this time."

A nice thing about renting a plane was that Brian didn't even have to pull it out of the hangar himself. The crew brought it right out to the front of the building for him. And they pushed his wheelchair back to the building for him, too.

Brian settled himself into the pilot's seat and flipped on the master power switches. The dash lights turned on. He slipped his iPad into a holster on the yoke and put his headphones on, then pulled Aviator Snoopy from his flight bag and secured it in the copilot seat.

He leaned out the door. "Clear."

The engine roared to life as Brian checked the instruments. After being cleared by the control tower, the Cessna took off and turned east over the city.

A voice came over his intercom headset. "Cessna Nine November Echo, we can't see you on radar, say altitude and heading."

What now? Brian shook his head and thumped his hook on the radio transponder that was supposed to transmit his position to the air traffic control radar. The little light that lit up when the radar pinged it remained dark. He scowled. You weren't allowed to fly without a functioning transponder in the Lincoln airspace, so this was likely going to be one short flight. "Cessna Nine November Echo is level at 3,500 feet heading one eight zero."

He waited for the order to return to the airport and land. There was a pause, then the voice came across his headset. "Cessna Nine November Echo, what are your intentions?"

"I wanted to do some sightseeing around the city tonight, Cessna Nine November Echo." Brian held his breath as he waited for the reply.

"Cessna Nine November Echo, traffic is light right now, fly heading zero nine zero at or below 3,500 feet, advise of your position and altitude and when you are ready to turn."

Brian pumped his fist. They were going to let him go! He repeated the controller's instructions into his microphone. "Zero nine zero at or below 3,500, will advise Cessna Nine November Echo."

He banked the plane to the east. In front of him, the dark sky shone with bright stars. Far on the horizon, the soft orange glow of lights from Omaha lit the sky. The city lights of Lincoln twinkled below him. Interstate 80 looked like two gold ribbons of light.

The Cessna passed by an empty but illuminated Memorial Stadium, home of the University of Nebraska Cornhuskers. Alternating stripes of light and darker green. Brian imagined the football field filled to capacity with a sea of red on game day.

He pushed play on his iPad, and music streamed through his headphones. The Cessna made a hard turn into the night as the engine roared.

Nothing but him, the plane, and the sky.

MODIFIED FLIGHT PLAN

The End

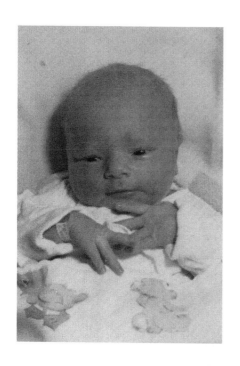

Corey and Brian Thomas

From L to R: Neil and Doris Thomas, Trish, Ray, Corey, and Brian Thomas

Brian Thomas First Solo
4-23-00 Inst. Tate Baloun

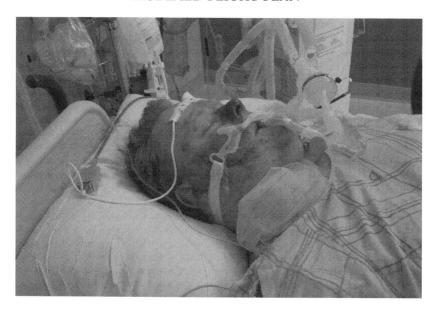

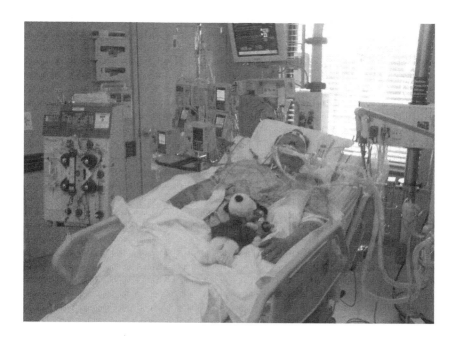

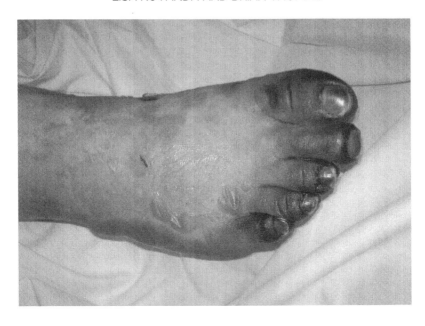

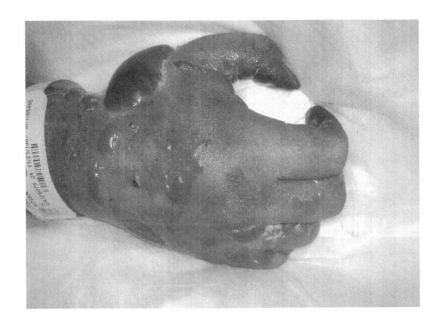

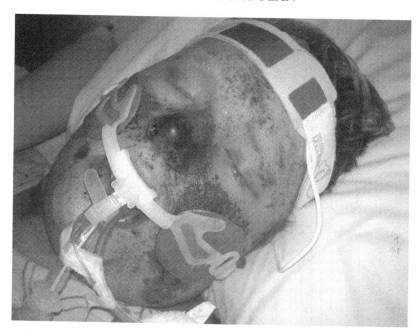

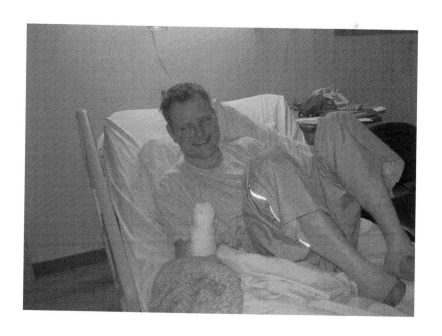

AFTERWORD

....

MEDICAL BACKGROUND

One thing that Brian and I have shared through the writing of Modified Flight Plan was a rather extensive knowledge of the disease process of Idiopathic Thrombocytopenia Purpura, septic shock, and the resulting sequella of disseminated intravascular coagulation or DIC–the illnesses that resulted in him becoming a triple amputee. While we've tried to keep the storyline focused less on the illness and more on the emotional journey of Brian and his family, we also recognize that as a reader, you may want to know more about the medical side of things.

I spent a good portion of my adult life in health care, so I know first-hand how horribly dry medical textbooks are to read. Trust me, the last thing I want to do is bore you to death after reading what is in my opinion an amazingly powerful story. But, in the spirit of enlightening and educating the world about a rather uncommon disease process, here's the scoop:

Idiopathic thrombocytopenia purpura is an intermittent bleeding disorder of undetermined cause. Platelets are a blood cell necessary for clotting. If you consider a clot to be like a brick wall that stops you from bleeding, platelets are the bricks, and clotting factors are the cement. A normal platelet count is 150,000-450,000. ITP patients can routinely drop down below 10,000. (Brian's record low was 5,000.) Normal platelets have a life of around 3-5 days, so they are constantly being manufactured in the bone marrow, and old platelets destroyed and removed by the spleen.

Idiopathic thrombocytopenia purpura is a huge medical term, so I'll break it down a little bit. "Idiopathic" means of unknown cause. Another name for platelets is thrombocytes (clot cells). So, thrombocytopenia means few platelets. Purpura are bruises, a hallmark sign of the illness. So, basically, ITP is an illness with not enough blood clotting cells due to an unknown cause, that causes bruises.

No one is certain why people develop ITP. The prevailing opinion is that patients first contract a viral illness, like a cold or flu. In the process of their body developing antibodies to counteract the infection, the immune system somehow decides that platelets are invading organisms and targets them for destruction. ITP is classified as an autoimmune disease for this reason and is not contagious.

The peak incidence of the disease developing is ages 1-6, however, it can occur in people of any age. Brian was two when he was diagnosed. The incidence is about 5 per 100,000. About a third of the kids who develop ITP will have one episode, then as quickly as it appears, it resolves. Sometimes without any treatment. About a third will have remissions and recurrences that last less than a year. The remaining third will develop chronic ITP and potentially have relapses the rest of their lives.

ITP is also associated with a risk of certain cancers, such as leukemia, lymphoma, and a variety of other health issues, many due to side-effects of treatment.

During the acute phases of an active bleeding episode, patients can have large bruises all over their bodies. Bleeding gums, bleeding from the gastrointestinal tract, and in cases where platelet counts drop to levels below 10,000, spontaneous brain hemorrhages can occur.

Treatment involves trying to trick the immune system into not destroying the platelets. Steroids, infusions of a blood product called IVIG, which is an immune globulin manufactured from donated plasma, and cancer chemotherapy drugs can help increase platelet counts.

Removing the spleen can help slow platelet destruction, but as Brian's case demonstrates, it places patients at risk of serious infections and may not improve platelet counts. The goal of treatment is to keep the platelet count above 50,000.

While Brian's case was certainly extreme, most of the time, ITP can be managed so patients can lead fairly normal lives.

* * *

Septic shock is a catastrophic cascade of events that occurs when the body attempts to fight an overwhelming infection. As the body attempts to fight the illness, a chemical storm designed to fight off the invading bacteria rages within the body. It creates side-effects resulting in multiple organ failure. The blood pressure drops, which causes reduced oxygen getting to the organs, so they begin to shut down. Lungs, liver, heart, brain, and kidneys can all be affected. The mortality of septic shock, even when treated aggressively, approaches 50%.

One would think killing the bacteria causing the infection would create a rapid cure for septic shock patients. However, particularly for gram negative organisms–those most often implicated in shock cases–the death of the bacteria can actually make the shock syndrome worse. The dead bacteria release chemicals that cause the sluggish blood to clot in the blood vessels. Once the supply of blood clotting factors–including platelets–is used up, patients bleed. It seems odd that in shock, a patient would have clots and bleeding at the same time.

This combination of bleeding and clotting is called disseminated intravascular coagulation, or DIC. The presence of DIC doubles the mortality rate of sepsis. Keep in mind, sepsis already has a 25-50% mortality rate on its own.

In Brian's case, the low blood pressure resulting in sluggish blood, and clotting of blood in his hands, feet, and face resulted in a rapidly progressing complex called idiopathic purpura fulminans. We've already talked about the words idiopathic and purpura. Fulminans means wide-spread. It can strike lightning-fast.

Within a few hours of falling ill at work, Brian had dark purple hands and feet, along with his nose and face. The mortality rate for patients with purpura fulminans approaches 90%, even with aggressive treatment. The dying tissue breaks down and releases more chemicals back into the bloodstream, which increases the shock cascade, which causes more tissue to die. A vicious feedback cycle.

* * *

I want to help, what can I do?

You probably don't have the means to fund major research projects for ITP, septic shock, or purpura fulminans. To be honest, few people do. But you CAN make a major impact in the treatment of these disorders, and countless others.

It won't cost you a dime, either.

Quite simply, go to your local blood bank or Red Cross and donate blood. Heck, if you're really poor, go to a plasma donation center, where it not only won't cost you anything to help save lives, they'll actually pay YOU. Each dose of IVIG used to treat ITP is made from the pooled plasma from over a thousand donors.

You read that right.

A THOUSAND donors.

That's not counting the people who benefit from the red cells, platelets, and other vital medications made from blood donations. You'll be saving lives.

ITP isn't all that common, but knowledge saves lives. Recognizing the symptoms–unexplained bruising and bleeding that may follow a viral illness–and seeking prompt medical care can ensure prompt treatment.

Want more information? Check out Abigail's Angels on Facebook, at http://www.facebook.com/abigailsangels, and the PDSA (Platelet Disorder Support Association for people with ITP) at www.pdsa.org.

AUTHOR'S COMMENTS

....

LISA KOVANDA

One of the first questions I'm usually asked as a writer is how I get my story ideas. There is really nothing magical about story ideas. They are around every one of us all the time. A random comment or image can spawn an entire world of fiction.

Stories like Brian's don't often just drop into your lap gift-wrapped.

I met Brian Thomas because my granddaughter, Abigail, also suffers from ITP, Idiopathic Thrombocytopenia Purpura. She was diagnosed when she was two years old, much like Brian. My daughter, Megan, quickly became involved in reaching out to other patients and families dealing with ITP through Abigail's Angels, a Facebook support group she founded.

Between us, we've talked to families all over the world who are also dealing with the consequences of the disease. Abigail and Megan are also spokespersons for the Nebraska Community Blood Bank, as they try to raise awareness of the need for blood donations. Every unit of IVIG, a first line treatment for ITP, requires over 1,000 blood donors.

It was because of a blood drive sponsored by Abigail's Angels that Brian discovered us on Facebook. Like every person who contacts us, I started talking with him–especially since he lived right across town from me.

It was then that he told me the story of how he had become a triple amputee. At that point, he didn't have his medical certificate to fly and didn't think he would likely ever get one. It was at best a distant "maybe" on his horizon. I mentioned that his story would make a compelling movie and book. We got to know each other over the course of discussing the possibilities for a script/book project.

It didn't take long for Brian to become one of my best friends. He's just that kind of guy. I had other writing projects I was working on, but we planned on tackling his story as soon as I could fit it into my writing schedule.

It was during November of 2011 when he made his first flight as an amputee pilot. I was sitting at Village Inn, hosting a write-in for NaNoWriMo, or National Novel Writing Month, which is a thirty day adventure that takes place every November, where participants write an entire 50,000 word novel all in one month. I knew he'd done his check flight that day, but when he posted the photographs he'd taken with his cell phone during his first solo flight on Facebook, I stared at them and started crying.

In public.

I typed below his photograph, "I'm seriously sitting here crying."

His response? "Isn't it beautiful?"

I couldn't even see the computer screen, I was crying so hard by this point. Tears of absolute joy at his success. I managed to get out a reply. "Brian, NOW we can make a movie."

I lost a mother-in-law and grandmother-in-law in a small plane crash in 1997, so the thought of climbing into any small aircraft was far from my list of things I wanted to do. But, how could I possibly say no to flying with Brian if I was going to write his story?

My first flight with him was a crisp December day in 2011. I'd known this guy for about a year, but while I was watching him do his pre-flight checks and pilot the Cessna we flew that day, all I could think was, "Who are you?"

I have never witnessed somebody so clearly in his element as I do when I watch Brian fly. I've since lost track of how many times we've flown together, but I'll never grow tired of watching him in the pilot's seat.

In the subsequent months, Brian and his family granted me amazing access to their most intimate and private thoughts as they relived his illness and recovery with me. I am forever indebted to them for simply being the amazing people that they are.

Usually, after doing all of my interviews, I hole myself up, churn out a draft, then send it off to the subject for their feedback.

That's not how it worked with Brian. We spent several weeks in either my living room or his, my laptop in front of us, and together we wrote the first draft. I've never offered to share writing credit with a story subject before, but realistically, Brian was truly a co-author in every respect. Not a word went on the page that we hadn't decided would go there together. There was no way I could claim this was all my work. So, the script of Modified Flight Plan is officially registered with the Writers Guild of America West with both of our names as authors.

Fittingly enough, one year to the month from when Brian took his first solo flight as a licensed pilot, I adapted our script to novel form for NaNoWriMo 2012. I do love it when life goes full circle! The first draft went to Brian for his additions of thoughts, emotions, and details, then we polished together, much like we did the script version.

It's hard to be grateful for the horrible things that happen in life. I'd take ITP away from every person I know who has it in a heartbeat. But, as the cliché goes, when life gives you lemons... I think we have made some mighty fine lemonade.

I love the story and hope it inspires you as much as it has me, but even more importantly, I've met some of the best friends I've ever had. To Brian, Ray, Trish, Dana, Corey, and your families... You will forever be in my heart and soul.

Love you more than you know.

AUTHOR'S COMMENTS

....

BRIAN THOMAS

Life has been quite the journey. Even though I've overcome so much along the way, I still sometimes struggle with pessimism.

It's been about four years since the whole transformation began. It's still hard to look back and admit what I've lost, but easier to think about what I've gained and how it all turned out. I get kind of scared every time I start coming down with an illness, like the flu. A reminder to be more diligent when I do.

There is no sign of the ITP returning, and I often consider losing my hand and feet to be an even trade to defeat it. With the hearing loss and uncertain future living this way, it's hard to be sure.

One endless hurdle I face is keeping skin grafts intact on my feet. I'm active, and the partial thickness grafts, about as thick as a piece of saran wrap, don't endure well. They wrap around the front to the bottom of my stump feet and bear most of my weight. It's mostly an inconvenience with discomfort until the tissue at the broken areas gets infected. Then, it makes walking extremely painful. At the peak of the infection cycle, I can hardly wear my shoes and braces.

I struggle to find a balance between being active at work and being active at home in my personal life. Nebraska winters are difficult. Snow covered parking lots make it virtually impossible to enjoy going anywhere. Decreased activity during the winters makes weight management difficult, which adds to the difficulties managing my feet.

The most frustrating invisible loss is hearing. Different voices have different effects. Soft spoken voices and high pitches are very difficult for me to hear and understand. Hearing aids are expensive, not covered by insurance, and only compensate so much. In noisy environments, such as restaurants, noise can easily overpower the person I'm trying to communicate with.

I try to locate my deaf ear away from them and have them sit in the corner with my best ear facing them. People most often approach me from the right side, and often I can't hear them at all.

My dad has a voice that is very hard to hear. In combination with the TV going and my mom's damn noisy pet birds, it's a lost cause. As much as I used to enjoy talking to and harassing my dad, much of that face to face communication connection has been lost.

Being physically disabled is not for the faint of heart. Fortunately for me, when my feet are feeling okay , mobility exists to adapt. The Americans with Disabilities Act was passed in 1995, and even though many improvements have been made all over the United States, I still often find more thought should be given to the topic. At old bars, hotels, restaurants, and places of business, it's not uncommon to find the wheelchair ramp way down at one end of the sidewalk and the handicap parking stall near the entrance into the building. A simple and easy solution of adding a ramp or grinding the curb into a ramp at the parking stall would cost very little.

I often find most hotels quickly sell out the handicap accessible rooms, leaving me with a regular room, hopefully on the ground floor unless there is an elevator. Often there is no handicap parking open at hospitals.

Most furniture has the controls on one side, usually the right hand side, which is great if you have a limb on that side that can operate it. Recliners come to mind. Trying to button a shirt or my pants can be frustrating.

Homes I can own or rent are very limited. Split foyer and multilevel houses are out of the equation, leaving ranch style homes. Since these homes take up more land to get equal square footage, there is often very little back yard space, or the lot is larger, which comes at a higher total cost of the property.

I often wonder why anyone would build dream houses that incorporate mutli-levels, lots of stairs, and tiny doors, as it makes retirement and living there into old age very difficult. Even old ranch homes often do not have accessible entrances, or a bathroom big enough to modify with a 36 inch wide door, or have enough room to easily maneuver a wheelchair.

There are often handicap accessible housing lists at local housing authorities, but unfortunately, they usually have a waiting list for rentals. So I was stuck with a 24 inch wide bathroom door in my apartment, meaning if my feet are infected I end up crawling on my hand, hooks and knees and/or taking pain medication in order to use it.

Winters dumping ice and snow on my car require a garage, and trying to find an attached garage on an apartment that is at least somewhat handicap accessible within my price range is not easy. I have not found one yet.

The remainders of my feet are very irregular shaped with bony projections requiring custom made foam inserts in my shoes. The foam lasts about three months, eventually compressing to the point where they hurt. It often feels like walking on rocks. The foam is on top of a carbon fiber plate that rests in the bottom of my shoe and is attached to the shin brace to give me balance and at least some support where my toes and forefoot used to be.

My right hand is amputated at the wrist, and the length from the elbow to my wrist is around 75% skin graft. I didn't know it at the time, but the skin graft on this arm was a blessing in disguise. Skin grafts don't sweat, so I'm able to wear a myoelectric prosthesis held in place simply by friction and suction. Had there been regular skin covering this area, the prosthetic would be built differently, as it would want to slide off from sweat.

Myoelectric means it's electronic and senses the impulses sent to the remaining muscles in my arm when I flex them to command the hook open or closed. So all I do is open and close my old fist. All the muscles are still there. It's a sweet machine when working well. I have yet to find a hand that I find as useful as the hook, due to durability and grip strength. Functionality is more important to me than trying to hide the amputation.

My left hand is severely scarred. It functions around 50% of normal range of motion, permanently contracted to a point where it makes lifting objects like a tall drinking glass difficult. Mugs with handles work best for me.

I chose to go back to work having nothing to lose, looking for purpose, and of course, income. By the time it was all said and done, my employer disability payments ended. I received a one-time sate vocational rehab grant which paid for a $900 hearing aid. I've never received any other forms of government assistance or disability payments. I pay approximately $5,000 per year, above what my insurance covers, out of my own pocket for my shoes, braces, toe fillers, wheelchair, hearing aid, and prosthetic arm. A high overhead cost to live.

Dating is what it is. Not much has changed since I was busy fighting the endless battles with health I've endured through my life. I never really had time to spend wooing women in my direction. Today, many confuse me with a war veteran and approach me in anticipation of hearing a war story. They lose interest after I politely inform them of their incorrect assumption. Some will start toward me, and after seeing my hand and/or hook, they look away and change course. Some are crazy, and freakishly attracted to me, while others just want to hear a good story.

Things happened during my illness that I didn't learn about until long after I was out of the hospital. I went around seeing all of my friends and family that I hadn't seen in years. This is when I learned how the whole event really affected people.

Two of my best friends from high school visited me on my deathbed and returned to South Dakota after saying their good-byes. They expected to see me next at my funeral. One of them nearly drank himself to death. The other broke down sobbing in front of me at a restaurant at 2 a.m. after a long night of partying together. He was so full of doubt concerning his own disbelief in miracles.

Everyone deals with tragedy their own way.

Finding new hobbies and things to enjoy is a big step towards moving on. Even learning to conquer the everyday things you once could accomplish without effort can be a rewarding game and something to take pride in.

As you grow and learn to adapt, the more accepting you become.

Hold onto what you can, and let go of what you can't.

Log online or go to local support groups for strength if you need it because you are not alone. Don't be afraid. It's just life. You can live modified, too.

ACKNOWLEDGEMENTS

There are so many people we need to thank, it's hard to know where to begin. First of all, we should thank each other. We managed to craft a movie script and book without killing each other, and that's always a good place to start.

Next, to our families, especially Brian's, who not only provided emotional support when we had moments of doubt, but who also bared their souls to help make this dream a reality.

To all the amazingly talented members in my writing group, The Local Muse, especially Gina Barlean, Kathy Gilford, Charlie Volnek, Belinda Kennington, Dee Feeken-Schmidt, and Mary Unger. We are forever indebted for your unwavering support and ability to tell us what we needed to hear to make this a stronger book.

To Local Muse member and friend extraordinaire, Victorine Lieske, we send a special and well-earned thanks. The fantastic cover design was a labor of love on so many fronts, and you brought it to life. That doesn't even begin to cover the endless questions, web design assistance, and general cheerleading you've done to keep us on track.

We are also grateful to the many members of the Nebraska Writers Guild who shared their advice and wisdom.

The fabulous Lisa Pelto, Nebraska Writers Guild member, and owner of Concierge Publishing and Marketing, for her experience, advice and encouragement.

Our wonderful editor, Cherise Kelley, who helped polish our prose, you are fantastic. If you need an editor, she gets our two thumbs-up. You can find her at:

http://size12bystpatricksday.blogspot.com/p/cherise-kelley-book-editor.html

Cover photography courtesy of Heather Waite of AfterImages Photography and Design. You can contact Heather at:

afterimage@windstream.net.

ABOUT THE AUTHOR
Lisa Kovanda

Lisa's first published works were illustrated stories her grandmother bound by hand into pasteboard fabric-covered books. A self-publishing pioneer before she'd reached third grade. After taking a thirty-year hiatus from fiction to raise a family, and a career in health care and retail, she returned to writing.

Her short story, "Curls of Gold," was awarded first place from the 2009-2010 Bess Streeter Aldrich Foundation.

Kovanda is a 2011 alumni of Lew Hunter's Screenwriting Colony. Her Colony script, "Til Death Do Us Part," was named a Top 25 Feature Script in the 2012 Slamdance Film Festival. It was also awarded the Bronze Oregon Screenplay in the 2012 Oregon Film Festival, and was a finalist in the Omaha Film Festival.

Lisa is the current President of the Nebraska Writers Guild, Municipal Liaison for the Nebraska: Lincoln, and Nebraska: Elsewhere regions for National Novel Writing Month, NaNoWriMo, and an active member of the Nebraska Writers Workshop, Local Muse, and a charter member of the Nebraska Film Association.

Lisa lives in Lincoln, where her canine companions and nine grandchildren occupy her spare time.

Other books by Lisa Kovanda:

Reckless Abandon

The Hunt

Cedar in Seattle

Available at all major eBook retailers.

lisakovanda.com

ABOUT THE AUTHOR
Brian Thomas

You've likely spent a few hours reading Brian's biography, and if you haven't we suggest you turn to page one.

This is Brian's first book. He's also co-authored the movie script based on this story.

Brian is a member of the Nebraska Writers Guild, Aircraft Owners and Pilots Association (AOPA), Experimental Aircraft Association, (EAA), Cessna Owners Association, Pilots of America, Aircraft Maintenance Technicians Society (AMT Society), and is a Certified Peer Visitor with Amputee Empowerment Partners.

authorbrianthomas.com

modifiedflightplan.com

MODIFIED FLIGHT PLAN